The Alchemy Spoon
Issue 2: December 2020

The Alchemy Spoon
Issue 2: December 2020

Editors
Roger Bloor
Vanessa Lampert
Mary Mulholland

A poetry magazine with a special interest in 'new phase' poets

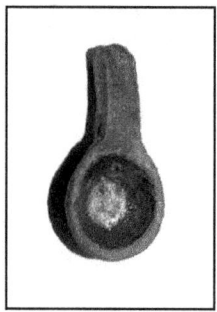

Design and production
Clayhanger Press

Typeset in Times New Roman

Copyright
Copyright of all contents remains with the contributors
Copyright for design and images Clayhanger Press unless otherwise stated

Poetry Submissions
Submission window next open from 1st – 28th February 2021

Please read the submissions guidelines on the final page
Submissions are through the website
www.alchemyspoon.org

Cover Images
Front Cover: *Metal* Diana Bell
Back Cover: *An Up day in Lockdown* Cass Wedd

Ring out the old, ring in the new,
Ring, happy bells, across the snow:
The year is going, let him go;
Ring out the false, ring in the true.

Alfred Lord Tennyson, *Ring Out, Wild Bells*

Contents

Editorial	Mary Mulholland	6
Scaffold	Ruth Aylett	9
Alchemy 2.0	Dave Wakley	10
The Gold Dress	Jane Wilkinson	11
Polishing the moon	Camilla Lambert	12
Cnut's mettle	Neil Douglas	13
Five Courgettes	Dominic Weston	14
Latin for Goldfish	Sarah Wallis	15
silver threads	Steve Harrison	16
Reassigned	Judith Wozniak	17
Ex Voto	Tamsin Hopkins	18
The dictionary concurs	Lesley Sharpe	19
Amalgam	Barbara Barnes	20
Printed Matter	Jane Thomas	21
Ode to Rust and Mould	Sue Burge	22
Bridges of Venice	Paul Stephenson	23
Double Chemistry	Matthew Paul	24
Fine hunter he wis too	Finola Scott	25
Copper	Barbara Cumbers	26
Roll Top	Kerry Darbishire	27
Savissick, Meteor Island, Greenland	Rebecca Gethin	28
Sodium Chloride	Rebecca Gethin	29
By-product	Rebecca Gethin	30
Rust	Diana Cant	32
While the Fruit Cake Cools in the Tin,	Ian Colin	33
Swords in the Rock	David Fleetwood	34
The Scolds' Bridle	Sharon Phillips	35
Urn	Susannah Violette	36
Weyland's Love Song	Ben Morgan	37
red plums at evening	Gillie Robic	38
Carte de Visite	Clint Wastling	39
Allez	Rachel Donati	40
At A Ceremony To Mark A Million Ways To Drive Small Creatures To Extinction	Julian Bishop	41
Late '80s Metal	Miles Salter	42
Zero	Ama Bolton	43
Furnace	Keith Tucker	44
Carving	Veronica Zundel	45
The Numismatist	Claire Smith	46

Cloth of Steel	Deborah Catesby	47
Virginity	Heidi Beck	48
Three-lettered	Simon Maddrell	49
In the silence of the beautiful white torpedo tube	Sara Levy	50
Scheelite	Philip Dunkerley	51
Carlos Acosta on the Tiles	Gillie Robic	52
A Lesson in Sodium	Dave Medd	53
Catching Silver	Chris Hardy	54
Revelation	Kathryn Bevis	55
A Personal View	Tamar Yoseloff	56
The Interview	Wayne Holloway-Smith	59
The Essay	Vanessa Lampert	65
The Reading	Niall Campbell	69
Reviews	Mary Mulholland Sue Wallace-Shaddad Vanessa Lampert	70
Reviews in brief		82
Contributors		88
Submission Guidelines		94

Editorial

'Oh metals metals, why are you always hanging about? Is it not enough that you hold men's wrists? Is it not enough that we let you in our mouths?' ~ Russell Edson

From the moment early humans first discovered copper around 6000BC, and gold and silver a thousand or so years later, people have been playing with metals. We explored their properties and qualities, marvelling at their strength for use in structures, utensils and vehicles, were awed by their beauty in jewellery and decoration, craved them for the monetary value we gave them. Metals are malleable, good conductors, lustrous. And excellent metaphors for poetry.

Plato described the highest level of human beings as gold-souled people who were endowed by nature with leadership abilities, silver-souled were the warrior class, while bronze-souled people were born to serve.

In alchemy, base metal is turned to gold. The four stages of transformation, nigredo, albedo, citrinitas and rubedo, were seen by Jung as a metaphorical parallel to spiritual evolvement and are used in transpersonal psychotherapy to represent stages of enlightenment. These stages also find parallels in how we write and craft our poems, from raw early scribblings to their finished burnished state.

In Chinese medicine, the metal person is patient, good, strong-willed. Metal governs the lungs, large intestine, skin, and relates to grief, courage and letting go. It also has an affinity with the element of autumn, and as we near the end of our Gregorian year, which is also the year of the Metal Rat (after which we will move into a Gold Ox year) it seemed fitting that metal be given a chance to shine in your poems, and what a rich selection you submitted.

In poetry we seek ever new ways to re-create and re-present experiences, to nuance feelings to convey precisely 'how it was'. Abstract words, such as joy, are often condemned in creative writing classes as inadequately expressing meaning, what sadness feels like to me is unlikely to be how it feels to you. There may be two thousand ways to express an emotion. Take love: it might be a casual end to a letter, a parent holding a dying child, the obsession of a first romance. The complexity it encompasses is considered by Wayne Holloway-Smith as he explains why he chose the title *Love Minus Love* for his second collection, which is currently shortlisted for the TS Eliot prize. You can read his inspiring interview on page 59.

The rich and diverse poems we received are also testimony to the ongoing proliferation of poetry in these unsettling Covid days. As if poetry reflects ever more powerfully our need to look deeper, to find meaning in life, to reconcile us with grief and tragedy, open ourselves to new ways of being, and hold onto hope in the face of the pandemic and what we have done and continue to do to our planet. In these times when many religions, the etymology of which is 'a way of life', fail the needs of our daily life and show a big decline in church numbers, we have not ceased to seek answers from a spiritual dimension. Poetry can offer solace. And poetry is flourishing, not just online but with wonderful new books being published every week. You can read Tamar Yoseloff's fascinating experiences of starting up a publishing house, her award-winning Hercules Press, in her warm and insightful essay on page 56.

Poetry often stems from the unconscious and dreamworld which offer image over language. Similarly, as Russell Edson says, 'Poetry is never comfortable in language because the unconscious doesn't know how to speak.'[1] Language is consciousness, and to a large extent how we communicate. In effect poetry is the meeting of the conscious and unconscious realms. In poetry, if not in speech, so much depends on the crafting and on precision. Comparing a first draft with a fully-formed poem is like comparing metal in its raw state with a Richard Serra, a Fabergé gold ring, a Tesla car, NASA's SLS. An equally powerful metaphor is provided by water, and in Vanessa Lampert's percipient close reading of a poem by Niall Campbell she examines how such crafting is done and what decisions might be taken. You can read her inspiring essay on page 65. A link to the video of Niall Campbell reading, 'The Letter Always Arrives at its Destination', can be found on page 69.

Between Diana Bell's front cover depicting metal's strength and Cass Wedd's back cover showing our human vulnerability you can read nearly fifty wonderful poems. And what a journey these poems take us on: someone is polishing the moon, a patient is realigned with titanium mesh, a speculum is 'shoved' up a vagina, a Christmas cake cools in the tin, we see a dress trailing surplus gold, a bicycle mechanic plucks spokes like a harpist. We encounter an argument in a cutlery drawer, sliced courgettes turn into sperm whales, we are in the dentist's chair, a chemistry class, we wear a scold's bridle, find a horseshoe on furrowed earth, remember a stilled moment in a car during a storm. We are an electric girl who is 'able with a blade', we're listening to Iron Maiden singing of genocide, sinking into a rolltop bath, dusting down a typewriter, seeing 'the cuspin moon', founding Norway, diving for coins, finding out too late the devastating side effects of tin-mining in Cornwall.

One thing these poems have in common is that they read as if they were written for us, the reader. As writers we are the observers. Only then we can hear in the silence what our innermost self wants to say and connect with that still deep place within, to write poetry the way, as Ovid describes, 'Brass shines with constant usage, a beautiful dress needs wearing.'

The Alchemy Spoon continues to be committed to supporting 'New Phase' poets, those who have come to poetry later or after other careers, but this does not preclude nor prejudice against other writers, young, old, of whatever ethnicity,

---

[1] http://www.webdelsol.com/Double_Room/issue_four/Russell_Edson.html

religion, sexuality, nor are we averse to experimental forms if they fit the theme. We are open to anyone who writes good poetry. What is good poetry? Glyn Maxwell suggests this is ultimately decided in the realm of dead poets [2]. But here at *The Alchemy Spoon,* we make decisions based on a communicated truth that touches us, unusual and arresting images that find new ways to communicate, an excellence of form (including free verse) and its fit to its content. Many other poems we received could have been selected, but decisions had to be made, and the final factor was how well a poem fitted within the arc of the other poems for this issue.

The next theme will be Spell, and once more we will invite the widest interpretations, which may take you into the direction of wizardry, etymology, alphabets, dyslexia, or farther afield. Keep an eye out on our website, Facebook, Twitter and Instagram for the next submission window.

Seasonal good wishes to you all. Keep safe in these troubled times, continue to be nourished by poetry and enjoy the poems selected for this issue – we did. May they sustain us all as we work our way through winter and look forward to spring, when, in Anne Carson's words:

> Out the kitchen window I watch the steely April sun
> jab its last cold yellow streaks
> across a dirty silver sky.[3]

Mary Mulholland

---

[2] Glyn Maxwell, *Drinks with Dead Poets* (London:Oberon Books, 2017)
[3] Anne Carson, *Glass, Irony and God* (New York:New Directions Books, 1996) p.15

Scaffold

Verticals placed onto wood blocks,
horizontals hammered in.
This is not an argument.

Planks, poles thrown upwards,
caught casually, clanged, laid.
This is not conceptual framing.

Their skill is routine, unshowy,
they do not surprise each other.
This is not a republic.

Cold metal drips with autumn rain;
with scaffolding up, roof-work can start.
This is not political metaphor.

Ruth Aylett

Alchemy 2.0

It is the metal season now,
Even the air turned sharp as a steel edge.
Outside, a silver birch auditions for an upgrade,
Its fallen coins scattered in the evening shadow
Of a moon as cold and blue as cobalt
Against a lead-black night.
Autumn's days are rusting, even the sturdiest branches
Brittle enough now to snap. Our streets
Are paved with gold and copper, phosphor bronze,
But they lead to the cemetery nonetheless.

In the garden, the ginkgos flare into sodium,
Butter-yellow leaves melting at our feet,
Winter turning treacherous beneath our step.
The love inside be what they used to call Greek,
Its bearers as English as raddled oaks,
But the hope, it seems, is Japanese.
Love's initial alchemy did not transform their basest materials
Thought its kindnesses flowed into waiting cavities
Like mercury into a snapped-tooth smile,
So they turn to precious metals to decorate the harm.
With time-learned tenderness, fingertips smooth lines of gold
Into their vessels' fractures with kintsukuroi's
Burnished kiss, and pause to pray such flimsy
Porcelain will bear to take the metal's weight.

Dave Wakely

The Gold Dress

O it was heavy. As though it had been
long hoarded in a burial mound,
when the earth doors opened, delight

was thinned a little by guilt, it was as if
the melt water of the dress's tread
trailed surplus gold, the meniscus

on the molten puddles shimmering
chemical tension, the net of knitted
metallic cords broke and re-wrote

the afternoon light into new lengths,
the handmade chainmail sheath was
medieval courage by way of Barbarella

via Courrèges, he said *I'd pay
one hundred pounds just to see you
wear that dress, even once*, quietly

in a richer voice than his own,
that came from under his fur
and muscle, these our first months,

when any chamber, any prompt
was a dress rehearsal, every plainsong
meal – oranges on a grassy knoll,

black coffee – was the wedding breakfast,
the first time we wed in St Michael's
Chapel, Canterbury Cathedral

completely alone so that God
could see us more clearly, pale gold
and fresh-woven like a willow basket.

Jane Wilkinson

Polishing the moon

She sits outside working at the silver, recalls
the legend of the moon storing what is lost on Earth:
vows not kept, hours wasted, unheeded prayers.

The spoons with their boar's head crests
take on a deeper shine, like the eyes-to-drown-in
of the man who left, taking her silver heirlooms.

A christening bowl remains, her aunt's name,
Selena, on the rim. She rubs off the tarnish,
moves on to a small hinged box. It once held

a moonstone bracelet made for a child who grew up
wishing her time gone, broke through every bond,
and fled one night when the moon was hidden.

Tonight the moon is crater-smudged, broken pledges
and rusted loves blown around the rocks, creamy,
not silver. She takes up the cloth, renews the shine.

Camilla Lambert

Cnut's mettle

Cnut
son of Sweyn Forkbeard
harried the Danelaw,
halved the apple land with Edmund Ironside,

married Emma, widow of Æthelred,
who grew him a harvest child.
So Cnut, believing himself
a Man,

failed to command the coming tide,
let the sea hounds lick his ankles – a plan
to prove he was not God.

Cnut, the skalds sang, removed his raven crown,
hung it high from the Christ tree, tongue-blood swore
to bear the ring-gold never more.

Neil Douglas

Five Courgettes

Five rigid courgettes
lie across the board
smooth Sheffield steel
marks and departs
each fuselage into
two equal halves

Limp-fluked tail open
to fist-tipped nose
a kitchen post mortem
of five Sperm whales
from east England's
winter beaches

Five rigid courgettes
are not the first veg
to summon up
kitchen cetaceans
melanzane prep
brings further deaths

As aubergine surgeon
I still and dissever a
plump pod of Orcas
deep marine flanks
reveal innards of a
startling Apple green

Dominic Weston

Latin for Goldfish

My father kept shares
in a Colombian Goldmine (*aurum meum)*

but wouldn't allow me to keep
a Goldfish (*carassius auratus*)

from the (un)fair. He saw no contradiction
here - and I would not see it until he died,

when his secrets caught fire in the light.

A 3000 years hidden Gold Bulla (*aurea bulla*)
surfaced in Shropshire (*Salopia*), UK (*Albion*),

decorated with solar fire (*solaris ignis*)
the imagery, the meaning, covered

over with tessellated triangles, (*tesselato stravit*)
centuries of secrets

come out dancing, come rippling the light.

Sarah Wallis

silver threads

Stainless steel spokes plucked by the bicycle mechanic
who trues the wheel like a harpist
listens to the strings
head pressed to tyre
for the right metallic ring.

She caresses the ornate *lugwork* on the second-hand frame
scoffs at the clumsy aluminium welds on the new imported stuff
laments the empty Black Country factories
turning out
hand-built steel frames.

Across the market
Music-shop mechanic threads the metal strings
chromed machine heads force the tension.
Eyes shut, he turns the winding pegs
like an antique clock
listens for the right note
plays the same old blues lament
to music made from silver threads.

A lug is a sleeve-like socket used in the brazing of the tubes to form a bicycle frame

Steve Harrison

Reassigned

I peer out through a slit,
breath brushes my lashes.

Rhythmic clicks count beats
with pulses of light

in a room without shadows,
ice white, steel-glittered.
…

Bound in my chrysalis,
of dressings,

I long for the velvet
touch of darkness.

I no longer own myself
—too late to unwind time.
…

Fractured fragments, pinned,
realigned, titanium mesh

sculpts who I should be.
He looms over me, whispers

Your own mother won't know you,
a glint of gold in his smile.

Judith Wozniak

Ex Voto

Find a photo of an underwear model, hips only. Cover with tracing paper and pierce her outline at regular intervals. Set aside.

Take a vintage tin bar plaque and remove the Jolies Bergères bloomers and high kicks with a wire brush. Use circular movements.

Wipe with white wine vinegar to neutralise. Lightly rub with steel wool to roughen the surface so the paint will adhere. Wipe again.

Spray with metal primer and when dry, paint with two coats of clear acrylic basecoat. Use a soft brush and long light strokes.

Prick out the model's traced outline onto the plaque by pushing a needle through the holes made earlier, filling the middle ground with her body. Add vulva details. Paint in flesh colour using enamel paint such as Yellow Ochre mixed with Metallic Silver Sterling to taste.

Using a fine synthetic brush with a seamless nickel collar, tattoo labia piercings and a swimming Koi carp in Ink Spot Blue across the mons pubis and lower belly.

Take a wider brush to make the background in Liquorice or Burnt Umber.

In the top right corner paint a floating head of Saint Kathy Acker, patron of unwanted daughters. Use Engine Red for the pouting lips, Baby Pink for the skin; mix one third Yellow Light with two thirds Wicker White for her hair.

Using the fine brush and in a cursive hand, along the bottom of the plaque write:

> *Because your God isn't listening.*
> *Because I don't know you.*
> *Because Pain is Interesting.*

Seal the plaque with clear varnish using light pressure. Heat to three hundred and fifty degrees, turn off the oven and leave to cool.

Hang in the place of your choice, hopefully where your mother will see it. The front door will be perfect.

Give thanks

Tamsin Hopkins

The dictionary concurs

You dare to do the thing that
unexpected, is hardly a surprise,
knowingly thwarting another
out of something that ought to occur.
And all the words I haven't said,
and won't, crash down with
the cutlery, silver in my hand,
steel cold. The knives' serrations
gleam, and the benevolence
you used to ease your guilt brims
in the brightness of the spoons.

Lesley Sharpe

Amalgam

Excess brought me here,
craving carved out an innocent pain.

His chair's professional tilt
cradles me, my hands comfort each other

on the rise and fall of breath.
We must be precise, this man and I;

between us a clever offering of silver
filings bound to curious mercury.

Together we hold the world still
while a single drop pools into place.

Cruel vapours begin their patient in-
filtration, new surfaces tempt my tongue.

In time poison may weary my senses,
unbutton my brain, but for now

I forget the threat of yellow-eyed demise,
test my thawing smile, my quicksilver smile.

Barbara Barnes

Printed Matter

The End.

Of hot type and your sharp metal thoughts,

all those fine words and slugs of cypher

crafted and cast from pigs of lead, and time.

Now it is the beginning of the cold.

Your galleys of tusche run dry over smooth stones.

creating confusion, smudges and letterpress doubt.

The familiar dance of smooth steps

       (upside-down / flip /

              backwards / off set / reverse out)

is now slow, considered, awkward and stiff hipped.

                                    Stray letters
The results are out of register, with ~~unreadable fonts~~,   blocks,

no binding, no proof, **over printing**, half tones, messages unclear.

Jane Thomas

Ode to Rust and Mould

O lickable rust with your bite and thrust   insatiable leech
you are my bit of rough   my pickable lust
powdering under the screet of my fingernail
praise be your stereoscopically observable scales
O my friable friend   my goddess dolled up
in leaping flame   to you I have sacrificed a lifetime of metal
O electron thief   corrosive chameleon   so easy to spot in a lineup
it's you   it's you   in your arsenic green underwater disguise

O then glory to the mould on my daily crust   penicillium blue green grey
of lovers' eyes   of stormy skies   pinprick schwartz on my shiny tiles
                              a million trillion unsqueezed blackheads
O splendiforous growth   speckling my jam like resting snowflakes
                   awaiting the sculp of my prising spoon
you yeasty moist-seeker   feisty fungal foo fighter
O the fuzzy microblombulous unstoppable sporiferous multitudinous mystery of you

Sue Burge

Bridges of Venice

Without parapets (no protection).

Without steps (you cross without realising it's a bridge).

Pugnacious (with white marble footprints and the starting point
for organised punch-ups between the city's rival factions).

With three arches.

That's also a church.

That's also a *campo* (one of sixteen *campi*).

That doubles as a road (a canal was covered rather than filled in).

Spanning several canals (two flights of steps and one level span).

A tight cluster (five, interlocking, and from them a view
of twelve other bridges!).

Offering the widest choice of directions (six roads lead off it).

Long and pedestrian (65 metres).

New (built for the re-opening of a museum).

That's only half a bridge (where you can step from one bridge
to another without touching the pavement in between).

That's a controversy (with its ribs showing).

The first iron bridge (1850).

Not facing the lagoon, but with a view of the Campanile.

The first stone bridge (for a safer journey after the assassination).

*Found poem from an article in a Venice Time Out city guide picked up
and perused in a room rented from a violin maker in Dorsoduro, Venice.*

Paul Stephenson

Double Chemistry

The hardest lads of 5N3 hold a smoke-ring competition
        at the back of the lab, toking away on Benson
                and Hedges sparked off the Bunsen

burners; while the rest, as always, toast squidgy pink
        marshmallows. In the moment Mrs Schwenk
                combines Sarson's vinegar with zinc,

Martin Lunt sits his grey-trousered arse on a white-hot
        marble nugget and howls like a werewolf shot
                through the heart with a silver bullet.

No-one comes clean; neither then, nor later, in the after-
        school detention. Not the next morning either,
                when Mr Claggett, the Head of Year,

his face already ketchup-red, labels us 'chinless louts'
        and, as soon as he's realised we're all in fits,
                'a rabble of unemployable shits'.

Matthew Paul

Fine hunter he wis too

Did you see it? Whit did he cry it?
Like oor flints ñ but shiny, sleeker.
At first dark when we gaithered roon the fire
eatin thon deer, the big one,
he cam in oot the woods, doon the valley.
We were haulin the meat aff the bone tryin
to chew the bigger bits
an oot the corner of my een I spies him
slide a wee thing from its hidie in his cloak.
Sic a bonny bone handle too
but what did he cry it?
The Blaed I think.

He broucht it to the haunch, sic a cuttin
edge like the cuspin moon.
Ane slide and there
there was a feather-fine piece o meat
lyin oan his cloak, a sliver.
We smiled welcome an wunnered
are there mony mair lik him?
When will they come oot the woods
and doon oor valley?

Finola Scott

Copper

And what of Lord Kelvin when he was Mr Thomson
telling the makers of a trans-Atlantic cable
that it wouldn't work? The wire was as thick

as they would afford and as thin as he'd said
it could be and still do its job shielded in gutta-percha
and iron stays, all carefully calculated.

How did he feel when he found he'd made
a mistake, that impurities in copper are significant,
that the metal they had used couldn't maintain

a signal for 2000 miles, that it would overheat,
that it would break? The ships still set sail, huge coils
unwinding cable that dropped softly into sediment

with the promise of America close enough to talk to.
Then waiting — the slow passage of ships
watched by fleets of lesser vessels, even though

he had stood in London weeks before saying
things are thus and thus, so it will not work
with the commanding air of a true prophet.

Barbara Cumbers

Roll Top

Rescued for a tenner from a scrap yard
rusty, still as a ewe caught in a drift of snow
waiting to be crushed, a body of iron
asking to be bought back to life, regain
    the same heat as the height of summer.

Once bathing was at the heart of civilisation
in ancient Pakistan, the hygenic thing to do
in the palace of Knossos, Crete, when tin
and iron replaced water-tight bitumen-lined bricks
    in rooms decorated with frescoes.

We fell in love many times with baths
corroding against hedges, abandoned by gates,
claw and ball feet standing their ground, overflowing
with spring water, dreaming their great weight
    lugged up a narrow staircase

to the luxury of inside plumbing, home late
from hedging February lanes, soaking our bones
in cast-iron-heat – a roll-top full
and steaming in a deep-limed room
    with a view to the meadow.

Kerry Darbishire

Savissick, Meteor Island, Greenland

This asteroid was a shooting star
and blazed across the universe
before its heavy fragments plummeted
into Cape York's permafrost,
shaping its snowland.

Inuit named each of the heaven stones
for things needed for their survival:
a seal-skin shelter, a woman sewing skins,
a sleeping dog – *nunatak,
ahnighito, mikkie*

The island was their secret treasure store.
Atomic bonds formed meteoritic edges
for tools once made from Narwhal tusk
and for blades to harpoon seal or walrus,
for needles, ice axes, flints.

Over centuries, the stones were hacked
for their iron, the snow all about
littered with hammer stones. If over-laden,
sledges could fall through the ice.

The whereabouts was finally given away
for a single gun. The meteorites were dragged
to *The Kite* through the snow by Greenlander men,
but it took a crane and twenty eight horses
to draw them through New York streets.

When hoisted into the city's museum
with no weather, no seasons
and only electric light
they became dumb stones, dead stars.
Like the five Inuit they enticed aboard.

Rebecca Gethin

Sodium Chloride

My grandmother held the licence to sell salt
legacy of a war widow's pension.
Customers would ask for a kilo or a half,
or, if money was tight
just fifty grams in a twist of paper.

She scooped grains of sea
from a sack brought up by mule,
measured the trickle of crystals
whispering into the pan
until the scales balanced.

Her salt was on every table
preserved meat and fish, blanched sheets.
She reared eight children during two wars
that were heard when the wind
blew thunder in their direction.

She kept soup on the stove
while husband and eldest worked the land
until the boys were called up
to fight in one war after the other.
Over time her fingertips whitened.

She could never wash away
the salt taste from under her nails.
When she woke she found more
and more salt grains in her eyes.
This woman of salt – quarried of tears.

Rebecca Gethin

By-product

He said *It's not till later in life
you notice* – the early deaths.
His old workmates, laughing in photos
from their mining days, are gone now.

In the graveyard, I see most men
died in their forties.
On tombstones the names
of infants are listed by age.

Tin mines run through here
under the cliff paths
like a lit fuse in a tunnel.

A grandmother's sorrow
runs in their veins like arsenic.

ii

It has no smell or taste
but turns your fingernails yellowish,
your breath garlicky,
and creeps through your system
sickening, blistering.
It could be food poisoning for instance.
You're on your own with it.

iii

Tinners' women knew the toxicity
of those head-turning Paris Green dresses
ladies loved to wear – they scraped
white arsenic powder from walls
of the labyrinth,
tying rags across mouths and noses,
handkerchiefs over faces,
slathering clay on arms and hands.
They'd squirrel a little into their pockets
to keep down the rats.

iv

When miners dug too close
to a disused tunnel
where a void had flooded,
and holed into *a house of water*,
the level filled in twenty minutes.
They never came home not even for burial.
Their widows at least had their work
in the arsenic ovens, deemed safer for women
than being underground. Their only hope
was for the foreman to take on the youngsters.

Note: Arsenic is a by-product of tin mining. Cornwall once produced half the world's arsenic which was also a constituent in a fashionable green dye called Paris Green. Arsenic is produced by burning crushed ore in ovens, then forcing the smoke through a labyrinth which leaves arsenic trioxide on the walls. Workers had to scrape off this deposit.

A 'house of water' is a miner's term for a void in a flooded mine.

Rebecca Gethin

Rust

Ground bruise-blackened,
soil hard-worked, furrowed,
iron on stone, scars of toil
on thin-skinned earth.

Two rusting ploughshares
pockmarked and pitted,
red ferric crumbling
of an old horseshoe.

Hidden in the brush,
an injured fox cub,
paw slashed on flint,
russet-red, alone.

How is it that a body rusts?
An overnight bruise,
a skin too thin, no longer
springing to the touch.

Diana Cant

While the Fruit Cake Cools in the Tin,

Mom gazes at the five-foot aluminum tree she bought
at the Five & Dime After Christmas sale in E-town.

Ain't this tree the prettiest thing ever, she exclaims,
fluffing out the shiny branches with tenderness.

I wish, I say, *we could crown it with a silver star.*
Entering the room, Dad shouts, *A goddamn fake tree.*

Take it down or I'll pitch out that piece of metal crap.
Mom storms into the kitchen to rummage in a drawer.

This year, she warns, waving the butcher knife she uses
to cut up chicken, *there won't be any tree thrown out.*

Dad grabs the car keys, stomps out the back door,
kicks the porch railing and drives off in the Fairlane.

I hand Mom her favorite gold and red tinsel corsage.
Her hand is shaking, so I pin it on her winter coat.

Ian Colin

Swords in the Rock

The clash of swords
Echoing off Hafrsfjord's walls.
Forged Norway.

Viking iron in hand,
Men of Hordaland, Rogaland, Telemark
Set out to test their mettle.

Harald steeled himself
Marched out in chainmail
To meet the Dane.

Silver gilded axe sang
Reverberating off stone.
Oak shields rent.

Men shattered
Mettle melted
Norway rose.

The battle of Hafrsfjord which many historians consider founded the country of Norway. The title echoes the monument to the battle which consists of two large swords plunged into the rock of the fjord - hafrsfjord.org/en/battle-of-hafrsfjord/

David Fleetwood

The Scolds Bridle

after an exhibit at Blaise Castle Museum, Bristol

It's him you picture first,
a big-bellied man
his arms scarred by burns,

he hammers iron bars
that glow pink from heat
curves them to cage

a head and face, his clatter
quieting to a thin tink
as the metal cools to grey

and he rivets the plate
to curb a tongue
then greases the lock.

His daughter is silent
in the doorway, her face
hidden by shadows,

breath shallow and quick
as he fits the key
and she hears it snick.

Sharon Phillips

Urn

I carry the memory of you
in an urn
upon my head.

The rust of it has dyed my hair
copper
like the river I loved,
and left.

You sacred python,
you and your scarred coils,
your effortless squeeze.

In that world I carried a sickle
used it as a moon,
keen with devious magic.

Stones on the riverbed
are slick, tumbled dark hearts
give up granite beats
to the rush.

In it, I am the amber
of long lost treasure
or iron after the rain.

Susannah Violette

Weyland's Love Song

Before we grow flesh, we are metal,
angular statues of light
in the house of the sun and the moon,

gathering, each of us, light
like a basket of flowers,
until light itself

usurps every colour,
a lily
on the face of the water

that falls to the seabed
as salt,
a star, old bullion.

I carve you, my love,
out of light,
my soul's knife gentle

and my fingers quick,
pinching your nose into shape,
smoothing away shadow, wrinkle,

lopping off errors:
the antlering wax on your forehead,
the droop of your wing.

Ben Morgan

red plums at evening

furnaces flame over flame
hairless forearms slick with sweat
shoot molten rapids
hard-hats
visored eyes
gauntlet hands
tongues working
the outside of teeth
clang
hiss
anneal
shift-change siren

donkey jackets
slant to the pub
serious thirst
nicotine windows
elastic smoke
overflowing ashtrays
coughs and camaraderie
saint sebastian dart-board
wrecking-balled skittles
pitch penny bench mark
hung up horse brasses
reflective glassware
a bowl of plastic fruit

Gillie Robic

Carte de Visite

Keep still!
watch the birdie!
Magnesium ribbon
burns and illuminates
as the glass plate is exposed.
Refined,
Cultured,
you stare back at me,
dressed in your Sunday best.
Silver salts fixed the image --
creating this *carte de visite*.

A butler once delivered your card
on a polished tray.
Were you kind, well-mannered, erudite?
Conform to all the social niceties –
sherry at 11, dinner at 8?
Your great, great grandchild
might be our elderly neighbour;
but all that remains of you is
this anonymous photograph
and for that, I'm sorry.

Clint Wastling

Allez

after Terrance Hayes

Ever-electric, ever-ready, everything girl
seeks boy for cutting edges, parries
& hits. Must be able with a blade.
Willing to whip & dress in white.
Should be open to play Rock
Paper Scissors Stones with steel
against flesh & bone. Must relish
metal masks & submit to body wires
for finely-tuned electric sessions of
long attack. Preferably willing to take
a beating – *en garde-pret-allez*
Should be comfortable in poules.
The broken need not apply
She plays to fifteen hits.

Rachel Donati

At A Ceremony To Mark A Million Ways To Drive Small Creatures To Extinction.
No. 999,999: The Tansy Beetle

Ladies and Gentlemen,   this last but one
entry demonstrates   man's breathtaking
ability for ingenuity in this crowded field,
home to the last   scraps of emerald tinsel
known as *the tansy beetle* – tiny metallic
lacquer-backed bugs whose foiled torsos
were excorticated   to decorate Victorian
cocktail hats –
                   thousands of wingcases
pinned by milliners   to ostrich-feathered
creations fabricated   from rabbit-furred
felt   as if the insect world were a creepy
crawly haberdashery   to embellish hats.
Such painstaking attention   to extinction
in pursuit of sequins!   It must make this
entry worthy   of the highest decoration.

Note: once widespread in the UK, the tansy beetle is now an incredibly scarce species only found in wetland habitats.

Julian Bishop

Late 80's Metal

'Is it heavy?' I asked, naïve, intimidated
by volume. My friend shook his head;
Bon Jovi's 'Slippery When Wet' was fine.

He passed me the cassette. I sniffed Richie's
guitar and Jon's drawl, and soon enough,
was hooked, buying TDK tapes from WHSmith

for the latest bout of home taping.
At Amersham Market, a squinty-eyed man
pushed me Magnum or Scorpions. Saxon sang

of 'Denim and Leather'. Iron Maiden told tales
of genocide to brutal bass. Def Leppard
had a lopsided drummer. There was a lot of hair.

At the end of the week, I'd get a fix of *The Friday Rock Show*,
when Tommy Vance's immense voice sunk
into my ears as he rummaged through tales of Lemmy

and Ozzy. My walls had acne: spots of blu-tac
held up heroes, I sewed patches (poorly) to my denim
jacket. I look back and frown at incorrect Whitesnake

sleeves (naked women seemed happy to straddle huge vipers);
these days, it looks more daft than thuggish. It's music
for boys, full of cowboys and guns, a soundtrack

for power fantasies. But certain tracks still kick the heart;
guitars point to adrenaline. Thin Lizzy and 'Don't Believe
A Word'. Have you heard that? I mean, wow. It goes like a bullet.

Miles Salter

Zero

the zero in my pocket
18-point Bristol
cast by Stevens Founders
from lead antimony and tin
has an honest face

damaged but not disfigured
it prints a uniquely imperfect oval
a character with character
twice my age
still making an impression

Ama Bolton

Furnace

I did not have a young man's fire,
the way my father had in his time.
Perhaps he had a dragon's breath fire in his Welsh feet
as he dashed across rugby fields, anywhere, any time;
His metal-studded boots always in the car *just in case.*
His sparking voice would arc bright notes into the air out of soft voiced choirs,
or throughout the burning passions of folk song groups.

I enjoyed the sport but my plastic studded feet always seemed earth stuck
and I had no iron will to run over the opposition.
I lovingly learned his songs, *Calon Lan, Ellen Vannin;*
But my tin ear always failed to find the key to their beauty.

Mother would mention the white heat of the furnace
each time we drove past the steel works; made sure I understood
that this was where my father forged our world,
where he returned from each day;
As if from a cauldron, white, hot, molten.

Keith Tucker

Carving

Start. Lift a wholly sharpened knife,
keen-edged by that weighty whetstone, grief;
after sighing, take a deeper breath:

accommodate your syllables to breath,
test the paring qualities of your knife,
severing skin from flesh, sinew from grief

– it's always in the bones you'll find the grief –
when all is flayed, nothing left but breath,
pulsing blood, sprung open by the knife,

sculpt the poem with knife, grief, breath.

Veronica Zundel

The Numismatist

Magpies cluster on Jack's
windowsill, tittle-tattle a black
and white yarn of feathered theft.
They tap beaks against the glass;

spy on Jack's spoils, chests
bloated envy. They swarmed
round him as he flew to earth
with a pouch obese with gold.

Their seven pairs of starved eyes
bulge as he unlaces, untangles,
exposes a first coin. He flips
it in the air, slaps it against

the back of his hand, spins it
in his palm. He strokes
the monarch's head, gropes
the rim, fondles the tail.

Claire Smith

Cloth of Steel

Thin as monk's flesh
ripped and delicate as air,
its few bright threads, metal
from armour, its back

flecked with cracks.
There's darning to be done;
when the light's not dim
strands can be stolen

from stiff edges. Use
your hands. They have grey veins
the skin is papery, the knuckles
lumpish, lines deep inside the palm.

Feel the rasp of the matter,
run your fingers lightly, touch the gaps.
How might the joins be made
new sinews fitted?

Deborah Catesby

Virginity

More and more women are requesting surgery to replace their hymens, in an effort to 'fake' virginity. But virginity is a psychological state, and a hymen is no reliable indicator it exists. (https://theconversation.com/reliving-virginity-sexual-double-standards-and-hymenoplasty-15307)

What I can't quite recall
about that time when I was nine
when he tried to jam
the swelling in his hand
up between my thighs, is whether
it went in, or how far, or whether
it only bumped harmlessly
against the entrance after all.

What I can remember
is the doctor nine years later
who spread my thighs on a table,
discreetly, under tissue paper,
though I could hear the metallic clatter
as he fiddled with the speculum
and shoved it in—my gasp
and flinch at the cold inner pinch.

Have you ever had sex? he asked then.
I don't think so, I replied.
Oh. Sorry, he said. *I should have been more gentle.*

Heidi Beck

Three-lettered

All that there's left is ivory seed
& breath's fluid, that hellish crimson ink
draws a life so poached & reproached.

Three-lettered iron reaching gut deep
love's purity now a tainted hemlock
steel rings chastise a poisoned zest.

Nightmares slip & slap too hard & dark a
shaman walking in ashen graveyards,
lesbians stroking bones that bleed.

Simon Maddrell

In the silence of the beautiful white torpedo tube

the scan begins. With NO ticked on the checklist for metal implants, coils, stents, I wait for the magnetic pull at a forgotten bolt, plugged deep in grafted cartilage, the bile retch tug and twist to loosen it and tear through flesh. Perhaps there'd been a childhood dash to A&E, some surgical repair to drill and pin a bone, long-since healed and never mentioned, my parents hazy on the details of which rough sibling pushed or which one fell. The machine creeps along pulsating veins, inspecting every organ, valve and joint. Eyes keen as a foreshore mudlark, sifting through the crimson wash and gristle for a glint of alloy plate or screw. No metal found, but still the tutting click, the slow insistence to scan each inch beneath the tideline of my body for what's amiss. And look, so small and deep we almost missed it.   There.

Sara Levy

Scheelite

A settlement named for a mythical saint,
a low hill rising from the plain.
Men came drilling, seeking their fortune
among the olive trees, without success.

Unable to forget the place, they went back,
reworked abandoned prospects,
lamped their way about the fields at night,
ghost figures jinking eerily over the landscape.

But it was in the coalfields they finally made good,
where a hard industry, once crucial, had died,
seeking with their black lights in the dark
the elixir, knowing it would be there.

Old miners, their lives streaked with grime,
looked on, curious, in stoic plight,
offered access to their one last portal,
secretly kept open, lit by tungsten light.

Philip Dunkerley

Carlos Acosta on the Tiles

Another tar-filled day tap dancing on sunbaked tiles.
Gouge, lift, chuck in rhythm, over the edge to tipper,
back broken bitumen, terracotta scattering
hard rain onto palms and pavers. Roofer hoofers

wheel barrows along the roof-ridge.
Forward kick – roll felt into place – retreat.
Forward canter – bang nail gun – retreat.
Forward mop – steaming tar – retreat.

Roof sealed and signed off, tic-tac routine.
Straw hat noon sky burns. Rest under truck
nested on unwrapped sweat cloths
and big plastic bottles of warm cola.

Tiles glide relentlessly from flatbed to roof
where one unhurries to retrieve a second's grace
before missed tiles fall, without breaking step,
lift and pirouette, dance to roof end stacks.

Conveyor retracts, lowers its neck to the garden,
broken flowers shudder back into silence.
Baked earth weaves across roof slopes,
intricate red braids tied up for the night.

Morning reflects in copper templates pinned
along eaves tiles rest on at the precisely right angle.
Roofers deft as casino card sharps, deal tiles,
flick flick into place, poker face display.

Gutters and ridges metalled, angles finger-clad,
clay-slipped, fixed and edged before a sheen of rain
settles the red dust. Shin down ladders, clean away,
time step the hot sidewalk, exercise at the bar(re).

Gillie Robic

A Lesson in Sodium

    memory fragile
    malleable
    ductile

the master dropped his nugget in our bucket

exploding water
sodium ruptures rain pearls
splits our meniscus

    it's elemental
    bending vision

a glittering gobbet to burst our potential

kept in a jar on the shelf
    our boy-bright pebble
drowned in glutinous liquor
    under safe oil

picked on a whim by clinical tongs
kids in a bundle wait on corruption
    by his wisdom

expecting to be rinsed in concentric ripples
    we leap for cover
caught in the tumult of aftershock
    his alchemy of laughter

Dave Medd

Catching Silver

Three ships outside the harbour,
two destroyers and a liner,
and my mother asking,
Who gives way?

Boys in the water
beneath the bow,
swimming amongst pipe fish
and spidery, green medusas,

shouting up for money,
catching specks of silver
that flash down in the sun,
in their mouths.

Men lying in the street,
who I thought were dead
but were asleep,
dozens of them,

and children who followed
with imploring hands,
shouting and fighting
when I dropped some coins.

Only later can you make out
how it all went together,
that what you saw passed through you
like a spear of light.

Chris Hardy

Revelation

Then darkness fell into the sky
faster than we knew how,
so we huddled close inside your car

which yearned to hold the conspiracy
of our breath against its windows,
and to hide us from each other

and ourselves, the way it does
when we sit not face-to-face
but side-by-side.

Then lightning cracked the sky
ajar and we saw the silver light
behind the world—so fierce

it seemed to see us back.
It's with me still: a fuse
that glitters every time I blink.

Kathryn Bevis

A Personal View

Tamar Yoseloff, poet and publisher, shares her experiences of returning to a world she grew up in

For as long as I can remember, I've been surrounded by books. My father was a publisher, and so the house where I grew up was stacked to the ceilings with leatherbound classics, crumbling paperbacks, and musty hardcovers with foxed pages. From an early age I was aware not only of the contents, but how books were made: I loved the proof sheets that showed colour separation in Cyan, Magenta, Yellow and Black, and the printers' samples of bindings and cloths. My father was keen for me to be part of the family business, and I worked in the London office for some time when I first arrived in the UK, but writing cover blurb and processing orders didn't thrill me; it was a stop-gap, until I could figure out where I wanted to be and what I wanted to do.

My leap into becoming a publisher myself didn't happen until much later, and it wasn't planned. My long-time friend, Vici MacDonald, had been taking photographs of London for many years as a personal record of things that interested her – shopfronts, street signs, dilapidated pubs, industrial units. She loved the same liminal bits of the city as I did, and I proposed a collaboration – I would write poems to go with her photographs, on the understanding that it would push her to present her work to a wider audience. As the project progressed, we knew we had the makings of a book, so I dutifully contacted a few poetry presses to gauge interest. I was surprised to find not many publishers were doing books that brought poetry and photography together, or if they did, the poems were added to enhance the photos, or the photos were an afterthought to illustrate the poems. As a graphic designer, Vici had already imagined how our book might look, and so we decided to publish it ourselves. Together, we fingered paper samples and chatted to printers, and the old fire that I used to feel when I was growing up around the making of books was rekindled.

We needed a name for our venture. Vici lived off Hercules Road in Lambeth, the site of William Blake's home at the time he was producing his greatest illustrated book cycles, so we felt 'Hercules' was appropriate; it was also meant to be tongue-in-cheek, as we were producing a tiny book on a shoestring budget. 'Hercules Press' existed already, so we decided on 'Hercules Editions', which had a classier ring to it. And we preferred the North American term 'chapbook' to 'pamphlet'. And so our press was born.

We launched *Formerly* at the Poetry Café in June 2012, alongside an exhibition of the poems and photographs. We then had a second exhibition at the Poetry Library that autumn. The Library generously gave us some funding to produce a map showing the locations in the book, so we visited all the sites (which took us two days – we're not sure if anyone else has ever followed suit), to see how they'd changed, and to chronicle our experience of going there together. We decided we would fill the display case in the library with objects found at each of the locations, and if we needed to make a purchase, then we would limit ourselves to something we could buy for £1. The most memorable find was a pair of ladies' black patent leather heels, discarded next to a dumpster under the *X-Zalia Night Cure* ghost sign in Islington (directly across the street from a funeral home). Many of the sites Vici had photographed were no longer there (and each time we went back, there were even fewer) so what started as a project to respond to each other's vision of London became a quest to preserve and record a rapidly changing city – an act of retrieval. I consider the poems I wrote for *Formerly* to be elegies for those lost locations, and I'm still immensely proud of what we made together.

Our little book would go on to be shortlisted for the Ted Hughes Award that year, and as a result, went into a second printing. We realised there was a market for books that brought poetry and visual imagery together as equal partners, each genre enhancing the other. So we decided to build on what we'd started, and find other projects that fulfilled the brief.

Fourteen books later, the press continues. Our ethos has always been to start with a poem or a sequence of poems that engages us in some way, and then to assemble a visual world around it. On a couple of occasions, we've asked poets to create their own artwork (as their projects were personal and individual, and seemed to call for them to extend the world they'd made in the poems). For some of them, it was the first foray into creating without using words. We often invite another author to respond through an essay that ties the images and words together or approaches the poems from another angle. We sometimes ask the poet to write something about the process of making the poems or we chronicle a conversation between the poet and the artist responding to the words. In that way, the book becomes a sort of kaleidoscope of different ideas and ways of thinking around a subject.

The books we make are modest, pocket-sized, inexpensive, democratic. We have received money from Arts Council, England, to keep going and rely on crowdsourcing and generous donations. At a time when it might seem books can easily be replaced by screens, it feels important to keep doing this. I made a move many years ago from reader to author and having had the experience of working with publishers from the other side of the process, I want our authors to feel engaged in the creative decisions around producing their books. I'm sorry my father isn't here to see that eventually I came around to working in the family business, perhaps not in the way he'd envisioned, but that the pull to be part of the birth of a book was inescapable. Apart from seeing my own words in print, starting the press is one of the most rewarding experiences I've had. I'm cheered by the fact that during lockdown, we experienced a spike in orders, proof perhaps that the screen will never completely win out over the printed page.

Tamar Yoseloff

Hercules Editions (www.herculeseditions.com) was founded in 2012. It has produced the following publications:

Formerly, Tamar Yoseloff (with photographs by Vici MacDonald), 2012
Heart Archives, Sue Rose (with photographs by the author), 2014
Ormonde, Hannah Lowe (with archive material), 2014
Silents, Claire Crowther (with film stills from the Cinema Museum in London), 2015
Hammersmith, Sean O'Brien (with photographs by the author), 2016
Rubaiyat for the Martyrs of Two Wars, Ruth Valentine (with paintings by Shahram Karimi), 2017
A Bargain with the Light, Jacqueline Saphra (with photographs from the Lee Miller Archive), 2017
The Singing Glacier, (with printworks and drawings by Emma Stibbon, RA), 2018
The Practical Visionary, Chris McCabe and Sophie Herxheimer (with artwork by the authors), 2018
The Gospel of Trickster, Nancy Charley (with drawings by Alison Gill), 2019
Cargo of Limbs, Martyn Crucefix (with photographs by Amel Alzakout), 2019
Veritas: Poems after Artemisia, Jacqueline Saphra (with paintings by Artemisia Gentileschi), 2020
The Wandering Mountains, David Wheatley, 2020
The Nine Mothers of Heimdall, Miriam Nash (with artwork by Christina Edlund-Plater), 2020

The Interview

Wayne Holloway-Smith lives in London. He won the National Poetry Competition in 2018 and The Poetry Society's Geoffrey Dearmer Prize in 2016. His second collection, *Love Minus Love* (Bloodaxe), is shortlisted for the TS Eliot prize. Here, Mary Mulholland talks to Wayne Holloway-Smith.

MM: Many congratulations on your new book, I'm really enjoying it and would like to focus our talk around it – maybe starting with your thoughts on titles – perhaps you can explain what's behind *Love Minus Love*?

WHS: It started off as *Love*, but I felt needed to be more complicated. Love, especially within an environment like family, can be complex and disruptive. You can have positive feelings towards someone in the abstract, while at the same time in the material and through your actions, be quite negative and disruptive. The title tries to reflect this maybe.

MM: One poem that springs to mind showing this is where you say, 'I found a small ring box/ full of my own milk teeth' near to where your dad died.

WHS: Ah, that's interesting.

MM: I'm also struck by the fact that none of the poems in the book is titled.

WHS: The book will probably split people because of this. A lot of people seem to want poems to exist as individual units, and I'm not into that here. Plus, I'm not keen on the idea of conventional narrative, nor the constituents a narrative requires – the way a character or subject is often necessarily reduced to a few recognisable tropes in order for the linearity to work. Narrative can't take into account all the contradictory notions of a complex individual.
    I wanted my collection to be a fragmented – 'one thing', but not a 'progression'. All the things are happening at the same time. I want the book to be read as a whole, with all the pieces contributing or gesturing towards this.
    For some people – it won't be their thing. One woman was complaining the book had 'formatting issues', because sometimes words are scrunched up together. I want to say people are allowed not to like it, but it's not because of a formatting or printing issue! This book feels like the most honest representation of my experience that I could come up with at the point of writing, and I'm proud of it.

MM: When the words run on it reads almost as if you are stilling time; in the opening poem,[1] it's as if you're saying we wouldn't be who we are without our

---

[1] 'Icouldbeafreegratefulguilt lessuprightsonandyoucould' in Wayne Holloway-Smith *Love Minus Love* (Hexham: Bloodaxe, 2020)

past, and our present creates our future. As if it's a book about surviving – in another poem you say 'my favourite word: alive.'[2]

WHS: I guess my favourite word changes depending on circumstances! But I see it as more complicated than the present resulting from past or dictating a future. It's difficult to put into words. Basically, I don't feel linearity exists. It's one way of conceptualising time, but as Zadie Smith talks about it in her *Intimations essays*[3], time is measured differently. Especially when you've got mental illness. One thought can last two weeks in terms of conventional time, meanwhile you're dealing with all sorts of other things, but this compulsive thought periodically takes over.

MM: Your poem about Krumme Lanke does this where you are both in that moment and observing yourself in the moment, then right at the end you say: 'I am laughing my whole self into my sad sleeve/at what this has so quickly become but wait: /I can come back from this.' In a book where there's virtually no punctuation this colon jumps out, adding something vital.

WHS: When Anthony Anaxagorou read this, with Raymond [Antrobus], on their 'Poems for a Lockdown'[4], he said, OCD can interrupt and ruin a really nice moment. And I think that's what this poem is: an attempt to resist and fight back against negative thoughts in order to enjoy a particular moment with my child. So I guess if the punctuation is doing anything there, it's really pausing all those negative moments to allow myself something positive. Or trying to.

MM: The closing words of that poem, 'the rhythm is in me', seem to refer to the front cover which shows a skeleton holding an accordion where the stomach would be. As if there's something particularly important about this poem.

WHS: Anthony felt that in a smaller context, in terms of its poetics, it demonstrated what the book does in a wider context.

MM: How easy is it for your poems to find their form?... There's a commonly held maxim that poetry is 10% inspiration 90% craft, is that true in your work?

WHS: I don't agree with that. After all, what is craft, and who gets to say? This book certainly doesn't conform to preconceived ideas of what poetry is supposed to be. It doesn't subscribe to traditional understanding of a poem, craft-wise. But I'd rather do what I want to do, and go where I want to go in poetry, instead of play to the perceived notions and traditions of British poetry.

And, how do we measure how a poem succeeds? If you are always looking to see if it does what previous poems did, in terms of line breaks, shifts, etc .... how do you break new ground?

---

[2] ibid p58
[3] Zadie Smith, *Imitations, six essays* (London: Penguin, 2020)
[4] Anthony Anaxagorou and Raymond Antrobus, *Poems for a Lockdown*, was on Instragram Live, 2020

MM: So would you say underlying your poems is a drive to be true to your authentic self? – In saying, 'the son could be dead and not know it', or stepping outside yourself at Krumme Lanke, you seem to be questioning your very identity...

WHS: I'm also not sure I agree with the idea of an authentic self. In fact, the level of fragmentariness in the book is my way of understanding this maybe: how we can think of ourselves as one thing while being several different ways at the same time? I think reduction in this area of identity can be very damaging. It comes back to narrative. And this happens all the time in politics: people are reduced to a small number of recognisable things in order to 'understand' them, constitute and control them as part of a particular narrative agenda. Even in my case, I'd be keen to resist the notion of one recognisable 'self'. I don't want to have to fit into an understanding of what a 'heterosexual' man from a working-class background is or should look like.

MM: So an authentic self ends up as a conglomeration of things...

WHS: Yes. But I don't think there is a vocabulary that's enough to accurately articulate anyone's life experience or 'self', with respect to body, mind and soul if you believe in all these things ...

MM: Looking at the covers of your collections, *Alarum* and *Love Minus Love*, there's a similarity – what is it about skeletons?

WHS: Twins!

MM: I notice there are also butchery references...

WHS: This makes me think of a few things. First, the idea of meat and the politics surrounding it. Rachael Allen talks about it in an interview with Lewis Johnson at Liverpool University[5]. I did one as well,[6] but she talks about these ideas more eloquently – meat as sexualised, gendered, politicised and class-based. And it always has been. Part of my decision in becoming vegetarian/vegan was to not partake in that anymore. The history of meat is about dominance. This raises ideas of privilege and priority, the rich get the choicest cuts, the head of the house (even in lower class families) traditionally get the biggest cut, while others had the scraps. And look at advertisements, for example, for barbecues – it's generally 'the lads' cooking steaks, burgers etc. One slogan for chicken, I think, has even said 'the way to a man's heart is through his stomach, unless he's vegetarian, then it's through his vagina.' One book I think everyone should read, one that made a big impact on me, is *The Sexual Politics of Meat*[7]. There's something about the class and gendered aspect of meat consumption, as Adams explains in that book, that I want to resist. But there's another issue with food in general: I'm pretty skinny.

---

[5] https://www.liverpool.ac.uk/new-and-international-writing/poetry-class/rachael-allen/
[6] https://www.liverpool.ac.uk/new-and-international-writing/poetry-class/holloway-smith/
[7] Carol J Adams, *The Sexual Politics of Meat* (New York: Bloomsbury Publishing, 2015)

I've had an issue with eating since my teenage years, and often it's been around wanting to take up less space. As a male I don't want to dominate. In effect, I want to reduce myself. I am quite preoccupied by it. So maybe the idea of skeletons on the front covers point to this.

MM: So you're trying to reduce the space the 'I' takes up? Perhaps you can say something about the 'I' in your poems?

WHS: People who have written really well about the Lyric 'I' are Sandeep Parmar[8] and Nuar Alsadir[9] especially, and most of what I learned, apart from what I intuited, the things I can vocalise about the lyric 'I' comes from them. There's a problem when we position ourselves as the centralised figure of the universe. The idea that I am in control of everything and able to tell you exactly what I think. That I have coded my 'message' through language in my poem and it's now up to you to decode it, and your reward will be you'll get my thoughts and teachings about the universe. I don't subscribe to this viewpoint. In my poems you will see the 'I' shifts according to different contexts in terms of time and space: sometimes it's a 'you', sometimes it's not me speaking at all. In the notes at the back I show some of the 'I's are from Kafka, bell hooks, Danae Clark, Jean Valentine's reworking of the Buddha's discourses, Jacqueline Rose, Richard Siken and Audre Lorde. All these people have been important to me and I wanted to give them space.

How people understand 'voice' is also interesting. Often people see a hint of this person or that in my work, but by including their actual words I am making it more into a conversation, I hope. Also, I wanted to show how 'my voice' could be disrupted by their voices, since they have all said it much better.

But there's is no point in pretending the Lyric 'I', doesn't exist. This is a book trying to work out how to navigate this issue. I think it's an honest attempt, and maybe some people will take it as inspiration and go and do something better.

MM: You seem to have a modest stance for someone who is a Doctor of Philosophy...

WHS: That sounds a nice thing, especially for someone who didn't get any GCSEs! My PhD is in English literature, but a lot of the texts I read were philosophy-based or cultural or social theory, so I was reading mostly academic texts, and thinking about class and masculinity.

MM: What made you go down the poetry route? I read that you started by joining a Roddy Lumsden class, with peers like Emily Berry, Inua Ellams, Ahren Warner, Amy Key, Mark Waldron....

---

[8]https://livrepository.liverpool.ac.uk/3009853/1/Sandeep%20Parmar-Bhanu%20Kapil.pdf
[9]https://liverpooluniversitypress.blog/2018/08/29/in-conversation-with-nuar-alsadir-on-fourth-person-singular/

WHS: Roddy had a big influence for quite a while. During 2007 to 2012/3 on most of the acknowledgments pages of books by young people his name would be there. He was hugely complicated but incredibly generous. All those people you mention were in his class... I started with poetry then went into Academia. I did a BA in Creative Writing at Brunel (having largely got in because of my age) and because I'd published a few poems.

MM: So were you working?

WHS: Before this I'd worked in a homeless centre, youth inclusion for a bit, was part of a Christian youth community during my teenage years... At my recent launch, Pascale [Petit] said she used to be a sculptor. I hadn't done anything in terms of art. I didn't even play a musical instrument. But when I went to Roddy's class, there was something there. I didn't enjoy a lot of poems we were looking at to begin with, but then he introduced us to the American poets...

MM: What were they doing that the UK poems weren't?

WHS: I found a level of excitement, urgency and risk in a lot of US poetry. D.A. Powell, Brenda Shaughnessy, Richard Siken were doing something special. Then in the UK, people like Jack [Underwood], Sam [Riviere]and Mark Waldron, Heather Phillipson, Kate Kilalea a bit later, made me think: 'Oh you're allowed to do all these other things.' Later, more poets like Kayo [Chingonyi], Inua [Ellams], Anthony [Anaxagorou], Ray [Antrobus], were doing stuff I admired, and I got to meet American poets like Jericho Brown, Danez Smith, Kaveh [Akbar]... It's not about thinking of it as a competition, worrying if my book will do better than that other book, but simply trying to take influence and inspiration from different voices. Hopefully we are all contributing to poetry moving forward.

MM: And breaking new ground.

WHS: Yes – otherwise it gets stale again. Will Harris is another really interesting writer. And I enjoy reading some of my students' work, even the really young people. I love looking at a new idea and pushing it.

MM: When you had a spell as poetry editor of *Poetry London* what made you choose one poem over another?

WHS: I was only guest editor for one issue. Being an editor, you have to find balance, and that's difficult. And you have to think of the existing readership, as they have expectations: certain names will attract a group of readers, exciting new names will be introduced. But for that one issue I could do as I wanted. I had to write the editorial, though, and that brought home the idea of empathy. Readers have empathy for writers: it's an act of empathy to take time to buy and read someone's work. But as poets do we always consider our readers? You don't want to be that person talking <u>at</u> someone, expecting them to take it all in, without allowing some kind of exchange, or giving that person time to speak, think. It's only fair both reader and writer get something. So, as a poet, it's about always bearing the reader in mind. Not with a list of bullet points, but to offer some wit, surprise, humour: that was what made me choose the poems I did. *Poetry London* has limited space for poems, whereas the amount of submissions I was getting wouldn't fit through the letterbox. It was a hard job.

MM: Your classes are always full, you have a loyal following, is there a secret?

WHS: I don't know. I just want to be generous and involve people, and for people not to feel excluded. I try to give away as many books as I can[10], and when I win stuff I try to put some money back into the community, as we all, or I certainly, have been in a place where economic circumstances preclude your involvement in certain parts of the poetry community. I'm grateful for people reading my work. Grateful too that people want to come to my classes. I worry a bit, don't want people only to listen to me. It's a bit of a dodgy thing when one person becomes centralised in other people's thinking as to what a poem should be. Part of my thought is to push some people out of the nest...

MM: Are you worried about becoming a guru?

WHS: I don't think I'm clever enough for that - haha! Part of the generosity thing is owning the fact that I have limitations, the same as every teacher or writer, and have my own aesthetic biases and there are certain peoples' writing I won't be as helpful to. I don't want people to think I have a catch-all knowledge, I very clearly do not. Sometimes I feel I'm guessing. Often I ask my peers' advice on how to teach or give feedback. I don't want anyone's investment in classes or in poetry in general to be wasted, or for people to think I know what I'm doing the whole time.

MM: Would you have a few final words for our readers?

WHS: Keep doing what you're doing. That's my message. There's no secret. There's no one way. So just keep enjoying yourselves if you're writing, and if you're just reading enjoy reading, and if you're buying my book, thank you! Read it as an experience not as a puzzle, there's no GCSE examination at the end, no right and wrong.

Mary Mulholland

---

[10] *Lasagne,* by Wayne Holloway-Smith was offered as a free download during lockdown

The Essay
More flow than ebb – the importance of liquidity in poetry

I have spent my life living as far from the sea as one can in Great Britain. Consequently, when the seaside appears before me, as I round a corner on a narrow road at the end of a long drive, I feel the same rush of joy I did as a child. There it is, mine again for a few days beneath its vast roof of sky.

In the summer between the two years of my poetry MA, I went on holiday to Cornwall with my seven-year-old nephew. Every day we would go to the beach, every day we played the same game as the tide went out. It struck me that there were parallels between our play and what I was trying to do with words, space and punctuation to create poems. I wrote:

'Around us is a flat expanse of wet sand patterned with rivulets and channels of water, drawn back to the greater body of itself. We dig, water collects. A pool becomes a lake, more water collects and overflows in streams through the sand, ribboning back to its source. We find rocks, pebbles and seaweed to reinforce walls. Our plan is to keep water in. We make dams inside escaping streams. Water rises; overwhelms our constructions, waterlogs and erodes, escaping where it finds weakness. The water outplays us, flattening feeble walls, breaching every boundary. We dig and build, stopping the tracks of water, engineers absorbed in our work, building our unwieldy failure, water always breaking for home.'

I reimagined a poem as a stream of words poets engineer to have the impetus to carry a reader down the page, just as water is drawn back to the sea of itself. A poet must manage the pace of a poem's delivery, crafting syntax and semantics to finely-tune this motion. Robert Frost said, 'Like a piece of ice on a hot stove the poem must ride on its own melting.'[1] A poet must train for the linguistic skill to allow the meaning they embed in their poem to travel beyond its black and white boundaries. A successful poem harnesses and translates into language, ideas about our existence borrowed from a great sea of human experience delivering them back in new formations of words, sound, patterns of rhyme, line breaks and punctuation. Poems mimic the movement of liquid and communicate what can create a feeling of intimacy between poet (via a poem's speaker) and reader, since poet and reader form a union when a particular poem carries *meaning* for them. Generally such meaning will be anchored in themes of love, family, work, friendship, culture, politics, nature and philosophy. Since meaning contains the emotional ingredients we humans crave, it is this irresistible feeling of connectedness that poetry offers. Poets seek for this to be felt beyond a poem's ending on the page.

I met the Scottish poet Niall Campbell when he read at an Arvon course. The poems in his first collection *Moontide* address his early life growing up on the Scottish island of Uist. They are beautiful in their gentle lyrical elegance and

---

[1] Robert Frost, 'The Figure a Poem Makes', *The Collected Poems of Robert Frost* (New York: Henry Holt, 1939)

additionally attractive to me because of my land-locked life and romantic notions of the sea. Here, reproduced with his kind permission, is one of the poems:

The Letter Always Arrives at its Destination

Then I wrote often to the sea,
to its sunk rope and its salt bed,
to the large weed mass lipping the bay.

The small glass bottles would be lined
along the bedroom floor – ship green
or church-glass clear – such envelopes

of sea-mail. Only on the day
of sending would a note be fed
into each swollen, brittle hull –

I had my phases: for so long
it was maps: maps of wader nests,
burrows and foxes' dens, maps where

nothing was in its true position –
my landscape blooming from the surf.
Later I'd write my crushes' names

onto the paper, as a small gift.
The caps then tested and wax sealed.
None ever reached my dreamed America,

its milk-white shore, as most would sink
between the pier and the breakwater
and I would find that I had written

about the grass to the drowned sand,
again; and to the sunken dark,
I had sent all the light I knew.

This is a poem both about the sea and *of* the sea; a metaphor for that which is beyond our understanding, existing before us and beyond us and holding what is known and the unknown with the reader carried gently and steadfastly towards its finale of mystery and magnificence.

Its first word 'Then' gestures to a time before the present, and by the end of that line, only six words later, it has reached all the way to the sea; compressing its own journey as a poem whilst simultaneously gesturing towards the human journey of a life.

The poem's regular tercet form has eight similarly sized pools of words, only the first and last lines of which finish with a full stop. Punctuation functions as pebbles in streams of words, instructing the reader to slow down or pause. Commas, at the end of lines and within them, are more pebbles slowing down the liquid flow, they are just a little smaller, so the interruption is minutely shorter. The two colons in stanza four are slightly bigger objects in the flow of text, requesting a moment's thought, perhaps a breath, but they are embedded within the lines so that the streams of words continue to flow past them.

Don Paterson writes, 'The last word in the line reverberates briefly in its silence.'[2] Movement slows because the eye stops momentarily. At the close of the first stanza in Campbell's poem that word is 'bay.' It opens the poem, in the imagination of its reader, to a wider expanse of landscape that encompasses land, sea and sky. The reader is carried forward by a desire for more detail; what did this speaker write to the sea? Hoping he will tell, we follow.

The reader instinctively seeks the convention of the full stop to mark the completion of a thought and is carried onwards through the quiet streams of white space between remaining stanzas by this desire to know.

Only four lines into this poem, the reader understands its familiar story of messages sent out to sea in bottles. The 'I wrote' of the first line offers the reader hope of a magical outcome addressing the freedom to imagine in childhood (still present, yet usually concealed in adulthood). The reader is captured by a feeling of having been recognised. The poet has further enhanced the fluidity in his poem by 'seeing' his reader, thereby creating a connection that the reader wants to keep.

Small cliff-hangers frequent stanza breaks, and these also pull the reader onwards: 'such envelopes' (of what?); 'and I would find that I had written' (what?).

In the sure-footedness of its title, this poem suggests a certain outcome (but certain outcomes are rarely encountered in good poems). Certainty in this poem is more ethereal or liquid; difficult to grasp. The poem offers acknowledgment of the universal child-dream of elsewhere and otherness. Additionally it addresses the contrasting themes of loneliness and longing for our secrets to be kept safe and treasured by another.

In the final line of stanza six, 'None ever reached my dreamed America', the reader is pulled through the open white space of the stanza break where the poem withholds a resolution and further arouses curiosity.

The final two stanzas are full of hopes dashed, yet not lost. In the words 'most would sink' and 'I would find', the reader surmises that the speaker's quest somehow continues. In the final line, the words 'all the light' meet the shoreline, the poem's last thought widening in its meaning, into new contexts that exist

---

[2] Don Paterson, *The Poem* (London: Faber & Faber, 2018)

outside its walls. The full stop placed here seems a convention, the feeling of the poem; its energy has built in its momentum and this overwhelms the last 'pebble'.

In her essay 'On Beginnings' Mary Ruefle says, 'the lines of a poem are speaking to each other, not you to them or they to you.'[3] I think this is the essence of a poem's unique fluidity. The poet cuts new lines in the 'sand'. The dam builders concern themselves with the ill-fated holding back, while the poem builders break forwards, interrupting their lines to keep them fresh, yet controlling their cargo of meaning in its journey back to the sea.

Mark Doty says the compulsion to write is 'a symptom of a problem of life having been not really lived unless it is narrated'.[4] As in life, the poem travels towards its own end. Poets position themselves near the beach, close enough to this 'sea' that they are able to gesture towards it while they talk about it. They tell stories of what this sea is made of, how it came to be, and how much more of it there always is. In so doing poets celebrate aliveness. This is their offering. Niall Campbell's poem is an exquisite example.

Vanessa Lampert

---

[3] Mary Ruefle, 'On Beginnings', *Madness Rack and Honey* (Seattle: Wave Books, 2012)
[4] Mark Doty, *The Art of Description* (Minneapolis: Graywolf Press, 2010)

The Reading

Watch the video of the Reading and Commentary
by Niall Campbell
on his poem

The Letter Always Arrives at its Destination

which you will find in The Essay on page 65

The Alchemy Spoon
YouTube Channel

https://youtu.be/mdzBL_AOxwE

Reviews

Mary Mulholland looks at a collection and a pamphlet from two poets who explore the impact of place on their lives as they reflect on the deep roots of what it means to belong and how at some level that connection always remains

Wendy French
Bread without Butter, Bara heb fenyn
Rockingham Press £9.99

Simon Maddrell
Throatbone
UnCollected Press £7.99

Hiraeth, a Welsh word for a deep longing for reconnection with spiritual homeland and ancestors, is the opening poem of Wendy French's *Bread without Butter* and sets the tone for this, her fifth collection.

Writing about a family past can veer towards nostalgia or sentimentality, but French's pared back writing avoids this, for the collection is more than a revisiting of a past, long gone, rather, it is a journey to see how the past re-presents itself in the cyclical patterns of family, and to recognise the importance of remembering and honouring what has been lost, and what we take with us.

The strongest and most enduring images of the collection come from the lost world of her Mamgu (Welsh for grandmother). These are warming poems with roots in stories passed down by the poet's mother, or in memories from her own childhood holidays spent at 'the small farm in a corner of Wales'.

The inclusion of two R. S. Thomas quotes about 'being' Welsh pays tribute to this national heritage, but it is the richness of French's largely autobiographical poems that speaks to me about belonging.

As the book opens we meet, not Mamgu, but her child: the farmer's daughter who became the doctor's wife, and learn about a thwarted love. This introduces a sense of loss that runs through the book, in poems telling of the death of a parent, the loss of Mamgu's world, the ultimate loss of place, language, identity. In 'Stories I heard while drying my hair':

> Fifty years on my mother longs for sheared wool,
> aches to caress it. In winter months she is her mother.
> Wears a coarse woollen cap.

Her mother, deteriorating through illness, becomes 'more Welsh' reverting to 'a language she'd never permit us/ to learn,' and her mother's death seems to be the catalyst for exploring this past. On hearing the plaintive whisper of her ill mother, *'rwy'n ar goll'* (I am lost) in 'And my mother is trying to tell me something,' French starts to revisit her family history.

It was a tough world where 'people got on with it', a world of bread without butter, where difficult or upsetting memories were relegated to the back of the mind. Symbolically, we first meet Mamgu 'on her knees' at 'Bwlchydomen farm, our farm':

> cows are milked lambs born men fed an old woman dies
> a child is born   a young girl suffering with tonsillitis
> has her tonsils removed   as she lies
>   on the kitchen table

The six-page sequence of Mamgu and Tadcu (grandfather) is like a tableau, with French's lyricism so vivid one can almost smell the bacon cooking as Mamgu in the kitchen tells and retells her stories to her 'peculiar London [grand]children'. Characters who inhabited that world are deftly brought to life: Natte the trapper, Dai the water diviner, '*Johnny bach* trudging over other fields'. There was a permanence and earthiness to this world, and 'Mangu knew God was Welsh.'

We can see her: 'Snow or scorching sun she'd wear her blanket /over shoulders, stride out to look at her *tatws*,' or, after dealing with the early lambing, preparing breakfast at the hearth for the men coming in from milking. This was a woman with inner strength but also empathy, who understood:

> when the harvest failed or a calf was still-born
> Mamgu would pack a picnic, and send us
> to Pendine for the day whatever the tide

Although we're told of Mamgu's dreams of being in a hotel 'observing the other guests in their finery, wearing/ her black skirt, white blouse and cameo brooch', we understand they would remain only dreams. She had no time for travel. Her world was the farm. Work was hard, but there was always a fire to keep one warm.

Mamgu's stories are interspersed with French's own childhood recollections. In 'Chicken Run', the narrator, a London child, has nightmares after being chased by a boy wielding 'a half-plucked, half-feathered chicken,' as the hens squawked in the background.

This world ends with Mamgu's death one Christmas. Recognition of precisely what has been lost is described in 'One Blade of Grass', when returning to the farm, the poet remembers being met at the station by 'my grandfather's horse and cart', finding Tadcu's handwritten notes of his cows, 'Albaertha, Aelwen, Deryn, all letters down to Wynn' and 'Me for once striding over this field wanting/ the dark to stay as it covets the silence.'

The next section of the book has a different atmosphere, more silent, colder, as the narrator sets off to Russia, Warsaw and other countries that would no doubt have bewildered Mamgu. We learn of a failed marriage, a child born, the death of her parents. Another but different brand of 'bread with no butter'.

This is a world where always 'It is cold'. In Warsaw, 76, 'the sky is a pause' and 'this is not home'. French journeys on, as she works through her loss, visiting her adult daughter in Japan, and here she sees through a chink in her daughter's bedroom on the wall, 'photos of haystacks, a farmhouse' (in *Keshite uchi wasurenai*). The past sparks to life. The narrator recognises, in *Grey*, 'I am the Mamgu now'.

The poet also portrays how the past can be powerfully evoked through random images. Thus, in 'Wiseman's Bridge', watching an old man slip on the pebbled beach the narrator remembers her father and 'a truth I once knew... in the ache of my body'.

French writes, in Mamgu's Room, 'no photographs remain of those days,' but these poems are snapshots, filled with such specificity and vividness that we can see:

> A lace cloth covered the table-top, a silver hairbrush
> she was proud to own and a jar of Pond's cold cream.
> *God bless our home* hung from a small mirror.

This is a warming and evocative read that captures the transience of time and place, while witnessing the evolution of family, and the need that transcends everything, to belong.

•••

Simon Maddrell's debut chatbook also evokes a strong sense of place and belonging: the Isle of Man, where he was born and spent his formative years. The curious title, *Throatbone*, relates to the bone that comes from the throat of the wrasse fish and is used as a talisman by fisherman and travellers.

How this relates to the subject matter of his pamphlet may refer to the importance of the throat in speaking one's truth, which can requires 'more spine than flesh' especially where it can be dangerous to own and be true to homosexual preferences.

Places shape us. We see ourselves reflected in them and in the families and people we encounter there, and Maddrell's chapbook portrays a strong sense of connection of and love for the Isle of Man. The opening poem, 'Threads' presents an island where 'stars spread a roof with planets for lamps' while inside the cottage, with 'a turf-cooked pot of spuds and herring,' we meet the 'shadows/ of a father before a child-bearing hearth,' and are introduced to the accepted ways of being on the island: smithy, farmer, or enjoying 'shed-fuls of gorse-flowered gin'.

That nothing is never just one thing is also reflected in Maddrell's compressed narrative, using language that is rhythmic and musical. There is beauty in the island's harshness, but a dark history too: 'On this island, blood courses moor, wood and sea/ glens sparkle and shade through hanging leaves' but there are also 'bitter rocks,' with Maddrell referencing in the same poem, 'Gravel Wrath', addiction and crystal meth. Life is complex.

The poems chart the narrator's life within this Manx landscape. In 'Bilberry Pie' he is a child for whom 'wild brambles were in my mind'. Maddrell refers to his child self and his father in 'Dinosaur teeth' as 'alien pods in a Pluto river' and, later, in 'Islands of Existence' he and possibly his father are 'two small islands chat beside the fire,' suggesting a subtext of isolation. For this is also the story of a man growing up gay in a community where homosexuality was illegal until 1992, and strong prejudices remained.

In 'Queer Courting', Maddrell questions the meaning of 'pure love' suggesting that depends on 'how you are with my *dooiney-molla* [man-praiser] and his kind':

>gods are walking in the garden like
>there are serpents in that red lawn
>now as common as fallen apples.

Maddrell's three-part sequence, 'Manx Pride, 1986-1992,' sits symbolically in the centre of the book, surrounded by the musical lyricism of place and everyday life. These three poems carry a different tone, angrier, more direct.

'*I would birch homosexuals*', Maddrell writes in 'Pride & Protests', quoting the chief constable, Robin Oake, at the opening of Tynwald in July 1991. The poem continues:

>Oake's stasi-style off-beat cops
>house raid & cottage arrests
>threats & promises of suicide left.

Another theme that permeates the poems is the metaphysical and what lies beyond. There is a sense that death, and its close association with love, is never far away, In 'Bay of Death': 'If this is *Pooil Vaaish* could/ I die just a little each dusk'. It seems the island is full of graves, and in his poem about the bronze age 'Meyall Circle', Maddrell uses a three-crescent forms, each subdivided into four, to create the twelve 'graves', which can then be read in several ways. This and other poems experiment successfully with form and white space.

The poems are multi-layered, and densely packed with references to folklore, nature, history and the environment. There are intertextual references to many Manx poets, such as T E Brown, W H Gill, Esther Nelson and Mona Douglas. Place names and Manx phrases, such as '*yn graih ma chree*' (love of my heart), add to the rich atmosphere and lyricism, and the music can be felt viscerally. Also from 'Bay of Death':

>silk-pooled bay
>thongweed floating soundless
>soaking seals, a rock teeth tease
>licked by waves, grasses brushing

These are brave poems, from a poet unafraid to share his struggles. In 'Black Dog' despite being 'stung/ by the howling breath of Moddey Dhoo' he is not prepared to live in disguise; in spite of 'castle legends torches burn dimly/ in dark passages where music has gone' he 'still looks in the mirror'. So when Maddrell says in 'For the Future Manx Poet':

> To unleash that red-billed chough, sing
> trench deep within the soil that bore you
> toil, toil, deeper than death,

he conveys the way love is complex, acknowledging that he has been shaped by harshness, yet beauty and truth. It is his 'island home of mindful rest' ('Island Home').

Throatbone is a wonderful journey through time, memory and place, allowing us an insight into what it means to be Manx, particularly for a gay man, particularly for one living with HIV, and to stand with this Manx shadow in these beautiful wild places.

Sue Wallace-Shaddad reviews two collections which share with us the colour of different cultures as well as vividly charting relationships and memories. She also briefly reviews a pamphlet focused on a highly personal journey of homelessness.

Arundhathi Subramaniam
Love Without a Story
Bloodaxe £10.99

Lucia Orellana Damacela
In*her*ent
Fly on the Wall Press £7.99

Benjamin Cusden
Cut the Black Rabbit
Against the Grain £6.00

Arundhathi Subramaniam has written a stunning collection which covers a wide range of topics set in a rich cultural context. There are poems about love, ageing, family, friendship, nostalgia and memory. For me, the book is about journeying through life.

In the poem 'When Landscape Becomes Woman', the eight-year-old child crosses a bridge of understanding, learning 'That mothers are women.' when viewing her mother through a keyhole:

> And that's how I discovered
> that keyholes always reveal more
> than doorways.

Subramaniam's poems about parents ('Parents' and 'Parents II') are insightful in the way they capture the complexity of the relationship in very few words. 'Parents II' shows how we are inextricably linked to our parents:

> They litter
>   your cells with memory,
>   your head with echoes,

The loss of her father and her love for him is explored in 'Finding Dad'. Subramaniam sets this in the context of understanding the parental role: 'parents were always / piecemeal'.

She vividly brings to life carefree times with friends in her youth, captured in holiday snaps, in 'Deleting the Picture', then recognises this as 'nostalgia', superseded by the reality of losing someone. The poem ends movingly: 'It would have been easier still / if you hadn't deleted the sun.'

The sequence of seven poems in 'The Fine Art of Ageing' is particularly striking. The poet distances herself using Avvaiyar (explained in a footnote as 'legendary poet and wise woman of Tamil literature') as the vehicle to explore ageing. In part 1, the language is succinct but heavy with the passing of time:

> But she knows the journey
> from goddess to gran,
> sylph to hag,
> prom queen to queen mum
> is longer than most,
> more tortuous.

In 'Remembering', we are invited to consider the nature of nostalgia, 'reflex, a spasm', and the nature of remembering 'more an instinct'. Avvaiyar is beyond nostalgia in 'The Fine Art of Ageing, part III'. She asks: 'what's left?' once 'nostalgia' and 'reminiscence' are gone: 'Perhaps just the oldest thing in the world – / love without a story.' This last line has particular significance as Subramaniam uses it for the title of the collection. It suggests love continues, even after our stories have finished.

'A First Monsoon Again' details nostalgia for the monsoon, with the evocative image of: 'a downpour of kisses / under a weeping umbrella'. The poet builds tension with a catalogue of nouns:

> the impossible nowness,
> the gasp,
> the sock in the chest,

Subramaniam often uses lists within poems to great effect. Her list of rhyming adjectives in 'Song for Catabolic Women', enhances her declaration: 'We're passionate, ironic / angelic, demonic'.

Interestingly the poem, 'Let Me Be Adjective', lists verbs and in a way that invites us to experience a relationship as if editing a poem: 'apostrophise, / parenthesise'. There is a sense of seeking, the desire to become something other:

> I suppose I'm asking,
> like the old bards did,
> to be your garland,

References to poets and poetry are threaded throughout the book, starting with the first poem' I Grew Up in an Age of Poets'. It is as if Subramaniam is drawing past poets into her conversations as she develops her poems. In the poem 'Mitti', she suggests poets have had the role: 'to be messengers / between moon and mud –'. The references, too, to goddesses and myths in many poems weave their spell on the reader.

Subramaniam writes in English but also includes Hindi words throughout the collection which helps root her poetic vision very much in Indian culture. We are also transported beyond India through the naming of different places. Each place brings its own otherness. Avvaiyar in 'The Fine Art of Ageing, Part VII' is: 'a traveller with an appetite / for conversation'.

'In Praise of Conversations' is a wonderful meditation on conversations that takes us across the world – to Yangon, Bombay, Accra, Cairo, to name just a few destinations. 'The Bus to Ajmer' details a tour to a shrine, with a very mixed bag of travellers, 'a circus troupe of a kind', including another poet, which ends 'The poet and I exchange addresses'. The names of poets and film maker listed in 'Missing Friends' add to the international flavour: 'kolatkar, pound, almodovar'.

Her poems tend to be written in short lines, often in couplets or tercets. This adds to the pace and emotional punch of the words. There are many beautiful images: 'a butterscotch moon' in 'The Fine Art of Ageing, Part III' and 'a thunderclap / of turquoise and tourmaline' in 'Part VI'. A sense of the spiritual is never far away. In 'The Strange Thing About Love', we read of:

sitting
under the stars

in ancient
bewilderment

'Afterword' brings the poems to a close. We return to Avvaiyar who anticipates her last journey. We are left with a feeling of mystery and wonder as we read: 'she might even ride / a Persian carpet to the stars.' *Love Without a Story* is a lyrical exposition of the journey through life; we are left the richer for having read these poems.

・・・

'Inherent' is defined by *Oxford Languages* as 'existing in something as a permanent, essential, or characteristic attribute'. The italics in the title of this collection highlight the importance of 'her' and the role of women in family life. It also signals what women can inherit and also pass down through generations. This is borne out in many of Lucía Orellana Damacela's poems remembering her grandmother ('Abuela' in Spanish) in the first half of the collection. In the second half, the poems embrace a wider range of subjects including the birth of her son, moments with her daughter and medical treatment.

In the first poem 'Beached Moments', Orellana Damacela poignantly interweaves childhood memories with the loss of her mother: 'She searches for her mother's gaze. / That gaze, she couldn't keep.' The poem 'Grinding' is also about loss, featuring the death of her grandfather, but the main character in the poem is the grandmother with her stubborn determination. The line 'With every turn she crushes the coffee beans further', encapsulates repressed grief. 'Knife Sharpener' provides an impression of the grandmother's way of life as she waits for the knife sharpener 'every Wednesday morning / with dull edges and cold horchata'.

I found the poem 'Break In' rather mysterious as it is not clear who 'she' is; it might be the grandmother again. The image of 'fabrics of decrepitude' is very arresting. There is a hint of a long life lived with 'the stage where she becomes indomitable, / splurges in old smells and words.' 'Abuela's Superpower' really rang true in its description: 'She eye-measured things with such precision / she knew at once where she could store them'. The final two lines of this poem are very evocative of the grandmother's life experience: 'Love, betrayal, pain, losses, illnesses, deaths, / she, the velvet-hands vessel took them all'.

'Abuela's Garden' is a beautiful poem, drawing a sensitive portrait of the grandmother's frailty:

> Back bent, hair tied in a bun, uneven steps.
> Smells and textures her garden Braille;
> the wisdom of her hands the main fertilizer.

The plant-related terms, 'withered' and 'stemmed', reinforce the way she is bound to the earth and its cycle of life and death. We are told, 'They inhabited her; 'roses, geraniums, / and wildflowers whose names scape.' The link to death in the future is also apparent in 'The Window' where 'Numbness in her legs, / she flower-gardens her universe'. Garden imagery is used again but with a hint of cemeteries: 'These grounds are not yet receiving / her biodegradable, ultimate present'.

'Embroidered Past' mourns the loss of her grandmother but takes comfort in an inherited object from her great-grandmother: 'Now I have, by way of my mom, / the embroidered linen your mother made'. The grandmother also lives on through remembered advice:

> You, who once told me that a woman
> is not a woman if she doesn't know
> how to make cheese, which I don't,
> but I could find out.

In 'Toast', memories stir again with the use of 'your white china': 'The tea set has held its own against the pull of time; / a ricochet to mindful crochet sunsets you enjoyed'.

In these poems we absorb the rhythms of another life, of another country (Ecuador). 'Sun Love' is a lyrical meditation on love using the words 'lemon', 'limoncello', 'lime':

> Melt a lime candy
> under the sun's tongue
> hyphenate kisses
> interlock shadows.

Common Spanish words feature in several poems. They slip off the tongue, lying embedded in the text. They don't need translation as we can guess their meaning – they have been absorbed. I love the use of 'una niña' (the girl) in The Páramo Train, with its affectionate connotations of the father-daughter relationship.

Orellana Damacela includes much shorter poems which have only six to eight lines; some worked better than others. In 'Drenched', she describes the moment of meeting her son at his birth 'his hair the soft blow of the most ancestral force'. In 'Something Borrowed', she realises, looking at her daughter: 'I don't have my mother's eyebrows; / I am just passing them along.'

Several poems toward the end of the collection are darker. In 'Sand Burial', the poet describes the 'rotten wooden body' of a boat which is 'Trapped like me.' In 'Satellite', we read 'The piranhas that hunt in my bloodstream / bite with the fluency of familiar griefs'. In 'Intruders', we come back to the theme of mother and daughter: *'Your mother had us too, do you remember? / You are so much like her, inside and out.'*

As we come to the end of the collection, two poems suggest a reconciliation with life. In 'Rain noir' the last line invokes 'The smell of second chances and redemption'. The final poem 'Ink-Carved Rusty Path' speaks of a journey, perhaps the poet's own bitter-sweet journey:

> to landscapes of words unknown,
> oxygen that gives life
> and oxygen that corrodes
> in every stroke.

This collection repaid re-reading several times as I found with each reading I noticed more of the subthemes inherent in the title. I particularly enjoyed the poems about her grandmother, but Orellana Damacela also shares much about herself as daughter, woman and mother in the variety of poems presented.

•••

In his very telling set of poems describing homelessness from the inside, Benjamin Cusden does not shy from difficult descriptions of feelings or circumstance.

Initially, Cusden builds up what we assume is his own life history. In the second poem, 'Cut', he explores the strains of his role as an editor using repeated references to the nursery rhyme 'See Saw Marjory Daw' to add to the sense of being out of balance. In 'First Steps' we share the shock of the bailiffs' arrival. The repetition of lines reinforces the opposing positions of occupants and bailiff. 'Bridge Maintenance' powerfully captures the deterioration in Cusden's relationship with his partner: 'our span ceased to connect the breach'.

At the heart of the pamphlet there are moving poems detailing the life of a homeless person. In 'I am Homeless Mornings', Cusden takes us from 'Town' to 'Countryside' to 'Sofa Surfing'. I particularly liked 'Doorways are for Daytime Sleeping' with its use of lyrical descriptions set in the harsh reality of night sleeping: 'to seep through unseen cracks, become less / than silhouette and feed your form to darkness'. Cusden describes the physical pain of hunger in Trixy Myxi: 'acid churns and burns my empty stomach bag'. The poet reveals his state of mind in 'Spring Comes to Suburbia' when the therapist 'stares as black rabbit burrows, burrows, / burrows digging deep deep'. 'Cut the Black Rabbit', the title poem, uses fragmented text which can be seen to represent breakdown and the disjointed black and white of a reality 'where all spent dreams scratch and bite'.

Cusden has written a thought-provoking, technically adept pamphlet.

Surefooted through complexity - Vanessa Lampert reviews pamphlets from two poets who explore themes of intimacy, family and definitions of femininity and masculinity

Isabelle Baafi
Ripe
Ignition Press £5

Kostya Tsolakis
Ephebos
Ignition Press £5

Isabelle Baafi has a command of considerable linguistic athleticism, both in of her choice of themes and in her willingness to embrace an ambitious variety of forms in this, her first pamphlet.

The witty and beautiful 'Endomorphosis' documents the speaker's struggle with her body;

> 'we – the soft on which the
> world lands-plundered dream of diets, detoxes, cells
> plundered. but wake up heavy, anchor, legion,
> hoard. We measure the past in inches'

She embeds this within the beautiful form of an outwardly curved right margin. This form triumphs over its content, wordlessly announcing the loveliness of its curvaceous 'body' in defiance of what the poem explicitly states in the language of its speaker.

Baafi uses a similar trope in 'hotboxing' where six columns of text, carefully contain a pared back and punchy story with the six columns carrying additional significance visually. Perhaps these represent the five people named by the poem (plus the poem's speaker) as they lie on a bed together (or perhaps the columns represent six joints). The white space pushing through the text both enhances the universal theme of our inevitable separateness from one another, but also unifies the characters in the story, intensifying their intimate bond inside the tight black spaces suggested by both the poem's form and its title.

These are poems that are witty, unafraid and hungry for intimacy. 'Ouroboros' explores the latter theme with its speaker performing sex acts before a web-cam, then later finding a boyfriend 'who tells me how relieved he is that I am not *like that.*' Once again the form of the poem enhances its theme by its shape, this one with a wavy left margin creating shifting uncertain movement on the page, the speaker is both one thing and another, one and the same person with the two versions of intimacy at odds with one another yet held in a unified form within the poem.

The theme of intimacy is a recurring one in Baafi's work, but where this is tender, the reader is not permitted to settle into an image but must encounter its shadow side, sometimes disconcertingly so. In the poem 'Caul', she offers the line 'Sometimes [....] you drape your arm across my shoulders. Nestle my neck in the crook of your arm. And always, somehow resist the urge to squeeze'.

• • •

Tenderness juxtaposed by harshness is also a theme in Kostya Tsolakis' first pamphlet. With its endearing opening dedication to his parents, the poet foregrounds that he wishes to privilege his connection to family. This bond underpins the speaker's narrative of a young gay man's life, first in Athens and then in London.

The first poem 'Bathroom in an Athens Suburb, 1994' closes with the words, 'as summer nears, it gets harder and harder/ to breathe': the speaker seems overwhelmed by sexual tension. The cultural norms of his birthplace, and his family's overbearing expectation and insistence upon heterosexuality has begun to feel suffocating.

At times Tsolakis's poetry is reminiscent of Richard Scott's, with the speaker studying images of classical statues, searching for their erotic potential in its opening poem, but overall these poems bear the speaker's suffering with less of a tough wordly edge than Scott's, and they often display the open vulnerability and sweetness of remembered adolescence. In 'First Time' the speaker says 'I'd expected lovemaking to be/a soft – easy affair/a seaside room,/the scent of lemons'

Tsolakis's poetry is courageous in its frank open-heartedness. The (presumably) translated material in 'Fragments of Emails from My Mother in 2011' name the poet affectionately with the diminutive 'iko' and in so doing, challenge its fiction and place its story directly with him. He brilliantly augments his poem's tenderness by the use of slightly unconventional syntax, mimicking the speech of a non-native English language user with the speaker's mother, simultaneously voicing deep maternal love and stubbornness.

> 'Kostiko/ only when you have a family and
> child/ will you understand how much we/
> miss you
> [.......] 'I'd love you even if/ you murdered someone/'

this deeply personal, fragmentary poem effectively increases the sense of pressure on the of the poem's narrator who is also the subject of most of the poems in the collection.

The next poem 'Nobody' shifts the reader sharply back to the private and risky world of the brief sexual encounter. This recalls for me Mark Doty's commentary on the risk and impact of HIV and AIDS upon his life and the lives of his friends. Tsolakis revisits this in the poem, 'Naming it' in in which 'we run out of paper/ to list our dead.'

If this collection is a 'coming of age', as described on its back cover, then this is felt most intensely in 'The Watch', in which the speaker sells his father's precious wristwatch, a family heirloom and 'The phantom shackle around my wrist'. This line encapsulates the powerful and liberating act of claiming one's own life so as to choose to live it contrary to expectation.

This is a wonderful collection embedding freedom, forgiveness and the hope of enduring familial love.

Reviews in brief

Sumita Chakraborty
Arrow
Carcanet £9.89

Sumita Chakraborty's debut collection, *Arrow*, takes us on a lyrical journey at times mythic, literary, autobiographic, but always spellbinding as she explores love, death and other meanings associated with *Arrow,* and creates an entire universe encompassing violence, abuse and environmental destruction.

The hinge point for the collection is the death of the poet's sister. In 'Dear, Beloved', she writes: 'Sister, when you died, your bones cast an enchantment./ We made a powder of them, and I named the powder *ash*,' Later, in 'O Spirit', she writes: 'I make a promise/ Someday, I will cause as much pain as I feel.'

Ambitious in its scope, we are led by an assured hand as Chakraborty dazzles us with image after image, playing with language, sound, etymology, and refusing expected endings. In 'Most of the children who lived in this house are dead. As a child I lived here. Therefore I am dead.' an image inspired by Foucault, she continues: 'Most of the animals who lived in this house are dead. As an animal I lived here. Therefore I am dead. The English word *planet* comes from ancient Greek and Latin words meaning *wander* or *wanderer.* '

As we wander through the poems it's hard to ignore the rich intertextual references, Louise Bourgeois, Wallace Stevens, Stendhal... One poem comprises found lines from her own translation of Rilke, and his quote sits in the centre of the book: 'You must change your life.' But this is not a book to deliver a neat ending. In the same poem she writes: 'a fable never *resolves* so much as re-declares its problems.' Instead she stands ' on the mountain that became my home' determined to discover new meanings, new possibilities, to keep alive a sense of 'wonder', which is what I felt left with after reading her book, dazzled by its images, such as, from 'Figure 11. New forms of physics and metaphysics': 'The alphabets, essentially, are trees.'

Lawrence Illsley
A Brief History of Trees
Live Canon £10

Lawrence Illsley's debut collection, *A Brief History of Trees*, is an exploration of grief surrounding his mother's death, as suggested by the epigram, 'You said you'd like to come back as a tree/ but never said which you'd like to be'. Each poem takes the reader on a journey of trees – beech, elm, sycamore, oak, holly, willow, plane and rowan, situating each in a particular landscape, Cornwall, Brighton, London and elsewhere, as the narrator's biography unravels, and he shares his anxiety that his 'novel wasn't moving.'

The book opens with, 'A mother beech, Tregeseal' in Cornwall, where the poet originates from, shortly before the death of his mother,:

> Both of us absorbed. Reading old fiction'
>   or watching television. The hovel
>   you called it. But it was home. More than room
> enough.

The language is both grounded, 'I walked - wrapped in old waterproofs/and inappropriate shoes,' and poignant as he encounters a lone beech which seems to parallel his mother and he reaches out to touch it: 'Togetherness and connection seem important to beech.' Personal narrative is interwoven with fascinating tree facts: 'the beech was called bōc, which became the word/ book, just as leaves became pages'.

The journey taken in the poems is reflected in the forms chosen, sometimes zigzagging down the page like an arduous road, or with words scattered like falling leaves. His mother appears in all trees: in Brighton, seeing a Cornish elm, he writes: 'Elms are like ghosts to me.' Later, at the funeral, in 'A pulpit oak and an organ, Pendeen', he writes, 'Grief soaked me. Struck me like a wave,' then, as if to tear himself away from emotion, he concentrates on describing the Holme seahenge, where once 'corpses were laid on the inverted stump of a giant oak.'

The last tree in the collection is, fittingly, the rowan, 'guarding the threshold/ between this world and the next.' However, Illsley writes, when he sees them, 'they only reminded me of the funeral when you were someone else.' This is an evocative and moving read, and a journey anyone who has lost a parent may recognise.

Vanessa Lampert
On Long Loan
Live Canon £7

Vanesa Lampert's debut pamphlet is a wonderful selection of heart-warming poems that are likely to leave the reader uplifted and refreshed. This is a poet who refuses to be brought down by life's sorrows and challenges, a confident voice, warm, humorous, unafraid. In 'Dangle':

> I wished for a compartment to ourselves
> would slide open the heavy door hopeful
> we might slip inside, so I could clamber
> to dangle upside down from the luggage rack.

Lampert tackles menopause, female body parts unflinchingly. In Canada, 'Nights when the moon's too heavy/ I think about my ovaries'. Family and love, with all their complexities, are dominant themes. In 'Toads', the poet finds the road is closed, yet is heartened that they, 'brought the street to life/ toads all roaring the same love me love me fuck me call'.

Each poem is a nugget of hope, reminding us that sadness and joy can sometimes hold hands: 'and this will be my freedom and I shall be its song' she writes in 'song of the rescued hen.' Lampert has a particular skill of tapping into the humanity deep within us all: in 'Margate in September', she and 'the boy' are on the beach, digging, and attract 'a tribe of diggers' building an island, with water all around:

> Everyone together,
> not digging now, but thinking our separate thoughts
> of all the things scared and incomplete,
> here's the marvellous thing we finished.

In this way the poet conveys poignancy without sentimentality, with line breaks reflecting mastery of technical skills. This pamphlet is an evocative, heart-warming read, filled with energy, spirit and humanness. The closing poem, about her father, somehow sums up the book: 'I looked up at the tower of him,/ and grief would never dare / to touch my life'.

Tim Cresswell
Plastiglomerate
Penned in the Margins £9.99

Tim Cresswell's *Plastiglomerate* is the third in his ecopoetic trilogy looking at man's impact on the earth. As a RAF child, and a professor of geographer, Cresswell loves and was formed by travel; as a poet he observes how the world is being transformed. 'Plastiglomerate' describes a type of frankenstein-rock appearing on shores, formed by plastic that has melted and merged with sand, shell, rock fragments.

His imagery is sharply observed, his language spare. In 'Nest Site Fidelity': 'Ospreys are back from /wintering in Aruba – //skywriting 'm's and 'w's.' In the city he describes in 'Car plant', nature taking over a Morris Minor called 'Bumble or Bramble', where 'Buddleia clings to the wooden trim', while he shows the irony of underground advertising portraying an idealised countryside: 'salmon /leaping falls,/a forest's bluebell haze.'

Cresswell's tone is never didactic, he merely tells us 'how it is'. So we hear about 29,000 floating bath toys, in 'Friendly Floatees/ Tripadvisor', released into the sea when a container fell overboard in 1992, and which continued to be found for 14 years.

'The Two Magicians' is a powerful retelling of a folktale which starts in a balladic, magical way with the transformation of a woman pursued by a man: 'she became a turtle dove /purring in the linden/ he became another', but descends into a horror story with DDT and government countryside acts destroying the countryside, while at sea 'the grey whale   sieving oceans' encounters only 'duct tape' and 'plastic - Misc bag material'. Ultimately man is 'rock fractured by high pressure liquid' while woman becomes 'earth tremors in the Norman Oklahoma.' The poem ends starkly: *'wondering what in the world did I do.'*

Cresswell's imagery is striking and memorable. From 'Legend': 'on some icy island beach/are whalebones, brittle, bleached under magnetic arctic skies.' This is a sobering, necessary read.

Sue Wallace-Shaddad
A City Waking Up
Dempsey & Windle £8

The poems in Sue Wallace-Shaddad's debut pamphlet are like miniature watercolours of the poet's experiences from living in Sudan and her association with the country in the 1980s and 90s. These are delicate, evocative poems, filled with colour and heat – and mouth-watering foods, such as 'In A Panoply of Sweetmeats':

> sugared almonds -
> silver and blue pebbles-
> on the wedding beach -

These colours evoke the opening poem, 'Meeting Point', of 'The White and Blue Nile' where Khartoum is located. In 'Treasure Trove' she described dates as 'necklaces/ of pale amber', oranges alongside 'emerald watermelon/ rind straining like skin-tight jeans. Place name and phrases enrich the poems and cultural details add to the atmosphere of daily life. In 'The Fisherman' a net is cast 'spreading like the umbrella/ of a silent jellyfish'. as in the sequence about a Sudanese wedding, where, in 'White Wedding Night', the bride is 'a shy girl':

> her skin softened and scented
> by performing smoky *dukhan*
> henna patterned on her limbs.

These quiet poems are of a life that continues beneath the daily bustle, and contrast sharply with a short sequence about the troubles in 2019 that brings us to the unsettled present-day reality in Khartoum. Yet in the closing poem, 'Donkeys and Dust' we return to that stillness, with a sense that there will always be 'two boys racing each other … in the dust-filled plain,' that hope is the talisman of the human experience. It ends with a vivid image of an empty bench, waiting.

Joe Carrick-Varty
54 Questions for the Man Who Sold a Shotgun to my Father
Outspoken Press, £7

Joe Carrick-Varty's second pamphlet reflects on feelings around his father's death. These poems convey a profound sense of loss and grief, but are also technical masterpieces, with interesting syntax and masterfully crafted.
	The untitled opening poem, 'here are the woods here are birds/ here is sunlight here is leaf and branch' gives a sense of what continues despite, 'no birds here is pool/look my father how he floats'.
	Much is conveyed by what is unsaid. A sense of the dysfunction in the narrator's relationship with his alcoholic father is portrayed as they watch football 'on his little settee that unfolds into a bed/in case you ever wanted to stay.' Later, in 'Withdrawal' the poet will 'Unpack tins of soup—open windows— scrape grease

from the hob—sync your breathing with his.' But death of a parent will always be monumental.

'The Children' carries the guilt of hindsight. The poet, watching a tennis match, with everyone cheering, writes 'this is not /a metaphor for grief' but:

> did I mention my dad has taken a
> shotgun to a field
> and I haven't realised because I am
> watching tennis

In 'More Sky' he passes a demolished building. He reflects on meanings and traditions of fatherhood, the titles reading like imagistic poems, for example, 'All my fathers are hunting dodos in the park'.

The title poem contains no question marks, suggesting all the questions he's left with will never be answered, and the end poem, 'Reflected on the TV /Calling their Dad,' hits the reader with a punch:

> I stand in a room and call my dad
> tell his answer machine not to worry anymore,
> that they have found his body.

This is a pamphlet where poems have been pared to their core, they are poems that will stay with you.

Martins Deep
A Sheaf of Whispering Leaves
WRR Chapbook series 2020

We were fortunate to have on the first cover for *The Alchemy Spoon*, a photograph by the Nigerian poet and photographer Martins Deep.

In this, his first chapbook, Deep weaves a tender narrative of poems, in the main addressing the loss of his father. The final stanza of 'what i wrote in my late father's shoes' reads:

> asleep, you steal into my head. through
> the dried, salty trails on my face;
> wear me my childhood body;
> fetch me petrichor in your palms,
> & speak in the tender notes of birdsong.

Deep's utilises his expertise as a photographer with sensitive visual descriptions set against the rich landscape of his homeland. He has a deft control of his poetry's 'lens', zooming in and panning out to keep his reader's attention. In the poem 'on black street: waterholes & wildlife', 'children [....] go panting this way & that; flaneurs with the red, smouldering ash of cigars glowing into bloodshot eyes drawn to everything with a danger sign.'

Here is a poet whose syntax is often unconventional, his use of language sometimes a little archaic. He regularly uses unconventional grammar. In 'bloodline of stone' 'everything/ has large mouths with the appetite of sinkholes.' This (accidental?) naivety frames the subjects of his poetry in unexpected ways. Its device additionally creates the sense that these poems come from a speaker who is young, albeit they are far from unworldly in subject.

In 'bedtime at sunset' 'a lyrebird mimicks/ the echoes of your father's regrets'. Deeps writes boldly of death and suffering but with an artist's eye for colour, mined from a rich culture. He is a poet who is bold in his willingness to experiment with form and metre. I look forward to reading more of Deep's work.

Contributors

Ruth Aylett has published widely in magazines and anthologies, including *The North, Prole, Interpreter's House, Agenda, Envoi, Southbank Poetry, Scotoa Extremis, Mancunian Ways*. Joint author of *Handfast* (2016), her pamphlets, *Pretty in Pink* (4Word) and *Queen of Infinite Space* (Maytree), are due out in 2021. www.macs.hw.ac.uk/~ruth/writing.html

Barbara Barnes is a Canadian-born poet and actress living in London. Her poems have appeared in *Poetry London, The Brixton Review of Books, Magma, Butcher's Dog, Ambit, Under the Radar, Perverse* and the first issue of *The Alchemy Spoon*. (www.barbarabarnes.co.uk.)

Heidi Beck emigrated from the USA in 1998 and lives near Bath. She wrote her first poem about ten years ago and is grateful to *Poetry Ireland Review, The North, Under the Radar, Brittle Star, Butcher's Dog, Finished Creatures, The Alchemy Spoon* and *The Live Canon Anthology* for publishing her work.

Diana Bell is an award-winning artist working across media including sculpture, installation, participatory art and painting. She collaborates with dancers, poets and musicians and has included poetry in her installations. Brought up in the West Midlands she now lives in Oxford and is a member of Oxford Stanza Two. www.dianabell.co.uk

Kathryn Bevis is Hampshire Poet, 2020, her recent awards include winning the Poets & Players and Against the Grain competitions and being shortlisted for Nine Arches Press Primers' scheme and the Live Canon competition. Teaching poetry-writing skills to adults in prisons, mental-health settings, and substance-misuse settings, Kathryn is working towards her first collection.

Julian Bishop is a former television journalist living in North London who is a member of the collective group Poets For The Planet. A former runner-up in the Ginkgo Prize for Eco Poetry, he's also been shortlisted for the Bridport Poetry Prize and is one of four poets featured in a 2020 pamphlet called *Poems For The Planet*. He's recently had poems in *The Morning Star, Finished Creature*s and the first issue of *The Alchemy Spoon*.

Ama Bolton is a writer, editor and book-artist and convenes a Stanza group in England's smallest city. Her poems have been heard at festivals, on BBC Radio 3's *The Verb* and on local radio, and have been published online, in magazines and in anthologies including Bridport Prize 2008.

Sue Burge is a freelance creative-writing and film-studies tutor based in Norfolk. Her first collection In the *Kingdom of Shadows* (Live Canon) and debut pamphlet *Lumière* (Hedgehog Poetry Press) were published in 2018, her second pamphlet, *The Saltwater Diaries* (Hedgehog Poetry Press), in 2020. www.sueburge.uk

Niall Campbell is a poet from the Outer Hebrides. His first collection, Moontide, won the inaugural Edwin Morgan Poetry Award. Noctuary, his second collection, was shortlisted for the Forward Prize Best Collection in 2019.

Diana Cant is a child psychotherapist with an MA in Poetry from Newcastle University and the Poetry School. Her poems have been published in various anthologies; in *Ink, Sweat and Tears, Nine Muses, Brittle Star* and *Finished Creatures*. Her pamphlet, *Student Bodies 1968*, was published this year by Clayhanger Press.

Deborah Catesby wrote plays which were produced in the theatre and Radio 4. She taught creative writing to mature students at Birmingham University. Having studied Fine Art at Worcester and Gloucester Universities, she now works as a painter (www.debcatesby.co.uk). She is a founder member of ArtWrite which brings writers and artists together (www.artwrite.net).

Ian Colin is an American who studies poetry in London, loves cornbread and red-eye gravy. He writes about his Southern and Midwestern roots. His poetry has been published in the UK and the US. He has performed his poetry at The Troubadour, Fourth Friday, Poetry at Three, the Poetry Café, and the Dugdale.

Barbara Cumbers lives in London. Now retired, she earned her living as an information officer in the NHS and as a lecturer in geology. She has had many poems published in various magazines and anthologies. Her first collection, *A gap in the rain*, was published by Indigo Dreams in 2016.

Kerry Darbishire lives in Cumbria where most of her poetry is rooted. Her two poetry collections: *A Lift of Wings* and *Distance Sweet on my Tongue*, are published by Indigo Dreams. She has won or been shortlisted in competitions including Bridport 2017. Kerry is currently working on a third collection.

Rachel Donati's work considers popular culture, sex, the feminine voice, family, violence & intimacy, 'a poetic beat and vocabulary that transports us into her world where it casts new light on our own experiences and sometimes can make us re-feel past encounters', Hazel Press.

Neil Douglas is a doctor working in London's East End. His work has been published by *The North, Hippocrates, Proverse* and most recently in *These Are The Hands,* the NHS anthology.

Philip Dunkerley runs a couple of poetry groups in the South Lincolnshire area, where he lives. He takes part in open mic events (when available) and his poems have appeared here and there in journals or online. Once upon a time he was a geologist.

David Fleetwood lives in East Lothian, nestled between the broad beaches and open skies of the East Coast and the rising hills of the Lammermuirs. His writing reflects these surroundings and a lifelong interest in the outdoors and provides a creative escape from his job as a civil servant.

Rebecca Gethin has written five poetry publications and has been a Hawthornden Fellow and a Poetry School tutor. *Messages* was a winner in the first Coast to Coast to Coast pamphlet competition. *Vanishings* has just been published by Palewell Press. She blogs sporadically at www.rebeccagethin.wordpress.com.

Chris Hardy's poems have been widely published in magazines, anthologies and online. He is also a musician, in LiTTLe MACHiNe, performing their settings of well-known poems at literary festivals in the UK and elsewhere. His fourth collection, *Sunshine at the end of the world,* was published by Indigo Dreams.

Steve Harrison from Yorkshire now lives in Shropshire where he worked teaching. His work has been published in *The Emergency Poet* collections, *The Physic Garden, Pop Shot, Wetherspoons News, HCE, Strix*, several on-line sites and is on YouTube as steve harrison poet. He performs across the Midlands and won the Ledbury Poetry Festival Slam in 2014.

Tamsin Hopkins returned to poetry after a hiatus of thirty years. Her pamphlet *Inside the Smile* was published in 2017 by Cinnamon. Studying for a Creative Writing MA, her work is published or forthcoming in competition anthologies, *The New Statesman, Finished Creatures, Best New British and Irish Poets 2019-21.*

Camilla Lambert began writing poetry after retirement in 2007. *Grapes in the Crater* (Indigo Dreams Publishing) was published in 2015. Individual poems have appeared in *Poetry Ireland Review, Acumen, Agenda, The Frogmore Papers, The Interpreter's House*, and *SOUTH*. She co-organises an annual Arts Festival in Binsted, near Arundel.

Sara Levy is a Welsh-born poet, currently based in London and studying with Newcastle University for an MA in Writing Poetry, via the Poetry School. She is a mother, wife and dog lover and works as a proofreader. Her poems have appeared in *Poetry News* and several anthologies.

Simon Maddrell, born in Douglas, Isle of Man in 1965, living in Brighton & Hove since 2020. Simon writes through the lens of living as a queer Manx man, thriving with HIV. His debut chapbook, *Throatbone,* is published by UnCollected Press in July 2020. *Queerfella* was Joint Winner in *The Rialto* Open Pamphlet Competition, 2020.

Dave Medd was born in Hull in 1951 and moved to Northumberland in 1969. His work has been published in *Poetry North East, Outposts, Orbis, Dream Catcher, Obsessed with Pipework* and *The Coffee House* as well as on *I Am Not A Silent Poet*. He now lives and writes in Rothbury.

Ben Morgan is a poet and academic based in Oxford, UK, where he teaches English. His first poetry pamphlet, *Medea in Corinth: Poems, Prayers, Letters and a Curse* was published by Poetry Salzburg in 2018. He has also published poems in *Oxford Poetry, The Sunday Tribune, The High Window* and *One Hand Clapping*.

Matthew Paul's collection, *The Evening Entertainment*, was published by Eyewear Publishing in 2017, and he is also the author of two collections of haiku – *The Regulars* (2006) and *The Lammas Lands* (2015) – and co-writer/editor (with John Barlow) of *Wing Beats: British Birds in Haiku* (2008), all published by Snapshot Press.

Sharon Phillips stopped writing poetry in 1976 and started again forty years later, when she retired from her career in education. Her poems have been published online and in print, most recently in the *Places of Poetry* anthology and *Ink, Sweat and Tears*. She lives in Otley, West Yorkshire.

Gillie Robic was born in India and lives in London. She is a poet, voice artist and puppeteer. Her poems have appeared in the UK and the US. Her two collections, *Swimming Through Marble* and *Lightfalls*, were published by Live Canon in 2016 and 2019.

Miles Salter resides in York, where he presents *The Arts Show* on Jorvik Radio and fronts the band *Miles and The Chain Gang*. His poetry collections include *The Border* (2011), *Animals* (2013) and *Fix* (Winter and May, 2020.) He likes cheese, Philip Larkin, and early Bruce Springsteen albums.

Finola Scott is Makar of the Federation of Writers, her poems are in anthologies and magazines including *New Writing Scotland, PB and Lighthouse*. Poems were chosen by readers for awards *at I,S&T* and *Orbis*. Stanza commissioned her work. Red Squirrel Press published her pamphlet *Much left Unsaid*.

Lesley Sharpe teaches literature and creative writing in London. Most recently, her poems have appeared in the *Aesthetica Creative Annual*, *Dragons of the Prime* (Emma Press), and *Finished Creatures*. She edits *Heron* for the Katherine Mansfield Society, and is a co-founder of Lodestone Poets.

Claire Smith writes poetry to explore other worlds. Her work has most recently appeared in *Corvid Queen, Illumen,* and *Spectral Realms*. She is studying for a PhD in Literary and Critical Studies at the University of Gloucestershire. Claire lives with her husband and their spoilt Tonkinese cat, Ishtar!

Paul Stephenson has three pamphlets: *Those People* (Smith/Doorstop, 2015), *The Days that Followed Paris* (Happen*Stance*, 2016) and *Selfie with Waterlilies* (Paper Swans Press, 2017). He was a Jerwood/Arvon mentee and did an MA with the Manchester Writing School. He co-edited *Magma* (issue 70 'Europe') and co-curates Poetry in Aldeburgh. paulstep.com.

Jane Thomas is currently working on her first pamphlet on the subject of Alzheimer's. This year she has had poems published in magazines including; *Stand, Envoi, ASH, Notes 62, Oxford Review of Books, ORbits, The Oakland Arts Review* and *The Oxford Magazine*. She was also commended in The Poetry Society Stanza Competition in October 2020.

Keith Tucker is a new phase poet living in Oxfordshire. In his day job he supports people with Learning Disabilities and Autism to use creative writing to communicate their needs, desires, and stories. He has recently been published by *Words for the Wild* and *Nine Muses*.

Susannah Violette is a Pushcart Prize nominee, has had poems placed or commended in the Plough Prize, Westival International Poetry Prize, the Frogmore poetry prize, CoasttoCoasttoCoast Pamphlet Competition. Her poems appear in various publications worldwide including; *Earth We Are listening, the Mountains You Cannot See, Channel, Cordite, Dreich, Blue Nib* and *Strix*.

Dave Wakely is one of the organisers of Milton Keynes Lit Fest and of Lodestone Poets, his fiction has appeared in *Ambit, Glitterwolf, Prole, Shooter, Token, Mechanics Institute Review* and *Best Gay Stories 2017*, amongst others. He lives in Buckinghamshire with his husband and too many books, CDs and guitars.

Sue Wallace-Shaddad has just completed the Newcastle University/Poetry School MA Writing Poetry. Her short collection *A City Waking Up* was published in October 2020 by Dempsey and Windle. Sue also writes poetry reviews for *London Grip* and Sphinx/Happenstance Press. She is Secretary of Suffolk Poetry Society.

Sarah Wallis is a poet & playwright based in Scotland. Recent work has appeared in *Lunate, Idle Ink, Crepe & Penn, Selcouth Station* and *Finished Creatures*. A chapbook, *Medusa Retold*, is due from Fly on the Wall Press, Dec 2020.

Clint Wastling's poetry has been published in *Alchemy Spoon, Dream Catcher, Dreich, Orbis* and various anthologies. Maytree Press published his poetry collection *Layers* recently. His novels *Tyrants Rex* and *The Geology of Desire* have LGBTQ themes and are published by Stairwell Books.

Cass Wedd had the space during the first lockdown to work on strengthening the parts of herself that she had shared with her late partner of 46 years, by making self-portraits. A long-time feminist, her work became the inspiration for a fundraising exhibition *Women's Lockdown Art*, for the charity Women + Health.

Dominic Weston produces wildlife television programmes, runs over the Mendip hills and writes poetry. His work often relates to family or the natural world, undercut by a healthy slick of darkness. His poems have appeared in *Agenda, Black Bough Poetry, Magma, The North, Under the Radar* and many other publications.

Jane Wilkinson is a landscape architect living in Norwich. She is published in numerous magazines including *Finished Creatures* and *Magma* and anthologies with Emma Press and Live Canon, she was shortlisted for the Alpine Fellowship Prize 2019, placed 1st and 2nd in Guernsey Literary Festival Poetry Prize and won Strokestown International Poetry Prize in 2020.

Judith Wozniak has an MA in Writing Poetry from the Poetry School and Newcastle University. She has had poems in *Ink Sweat & Tears, The Poetry Shed, The Hippocrates Prize Anthology 2019 and These are the Hands* NHS Anthology. She won 1st and joint 3rd place in the Hippocrates Prize 2020.

Tamar Yoseloff's sixth collection is *The Black Place* (Seren, 2019). She's also the author of *Formerly* (with photographs by Vici MacDonald), shortlisted for the Ted Hughes Award, and collaborative editions with artists Linda Karshan and Charlotte Harker respectively. She's a lecturer on the Poetry School / Newcastle University MA in Writing Poetry.

Veronica Zundel is a freelance non-fiction writer who has recently graduated from the Poetry School/Newcastle University MA in Writing Poetry with distinction. She has been writing poetry for 50 years and has had poems published in *Other Poetry, Magma* and several anthologies, and has won the Barnet and Cruse Lines prizes.

Submission Guidelines

We welcome submissions of up to three brilliant, unpublished, original poems on the issue's theme through the website during the submission window. You will find full details of how to submit on our website: www.alchemyspoon.org

- We are only able to accept submission from those over 18
- If you have poems published in the current issue of *The Alchemy Spoon,* then we ask that you wait out one issue before submitting more work.
- Simultaneous submissions are permitted but please tell us straightaway if a poem is accepted for publication elsewhere
- We aim for a speedy turn-round and will respond to every submission, but we don't offer individual feedback
- Authors retain all rights. However, if a poem is then published elsewhere, please acknowledge that it first appeared in *The Alchemy Spoon*
- Our submission window for Issue 3 will be open 1st – 28th February 2021, the theme for issue 3 is 'Spell'

Submission Guidelines for Essays
- If you have an essay on some cutting-edge poetry-related topic, please send it to us during the submission window for consideration +/- 1500 words

Submission Guidelines for Artwork
- We are looking for original artwork to feature on future magazine covers. Portrait-orientated images work best (or images suitable for cropping). Good quality lower resolution images can be sent at the submission stage, but higher res files will be needed (2480 pixels x 3508 pixels) at print stage

Submission Guidelines for Reviews
- If you would like to recommend a poetry collection or submit a review of a collection, then please email us or use the contact form on the website

Poetry Workshops
- *The Alchemy Spoon* editors offer a one-to-one poetry feedback and workshopping service without prejudice via Zoom or Facetime. All profits from this contribute to the cost of running Clayhanger Press. Please email to discuss this - vanessa.tas@btinternet.com

Print copies of *The Alchemy Spoon* can be purchased from Clayhanger Press

www.ingramcontent.com/pod-product-compliance
Lightning Source LLC
Chambersburg PA
CBHW050507120526
44588CB00044B/1673